GARDENS AND PLANTS OF THE GETTY VILLA

GARDENS AND PLANTS
OF THE GETTY VILLA

ESSAYS BY PATRICK BOWE

PLANT DESCRIPTIONS BY MICHAEL D. DEHART

THE J. PAUL GETTY MUSEUM | LOS ANGELES

Getty Publications
1200 Getty Center Drive, Suite 500
Los Angeles, CA 90049-1682
www.gettypublications.org

Gregory M. Britton, *Publisher*
Beatrice Hohenegger, *Editor*
Robin Ray, *Manuscript Editor*
Catherine Lorenz, *Designer*
Anita Keys, *Production Coordinator*

Photography by Ellen M. Rosenbery, Tahnee L. Cracchiola,
and Lisa Talbot
Separations by Professional Graphics Inc.,
Rockford, Illinois
Printed and bound by Tien Wah Press, Singapore

Library of Congress Cataloging-in-Publication Data

Bowe, Patrick.
  Gardens and plants of the Getty Villa / essays by Patrick
Bowe ; plant descriptions by Michael D. DeHart.
    p. cm.
  Includes bibliographical references and index.
  ISBN 978-1-60606-049-0 (softcover)
  1. Gardens, Roman—California—Malibu. 2. Plants,
Ornamental—California—Malibu. 3. Getty Villa (Malibu,
Calif.) I. DeHart, Michael D. II. Title.
  SB466.U7G482 2011
  712'.60979494—dc22
                    2010034498

ACKNOWLEDGMENTS

I would like to thank Tahnee L. Cracchiola, Benedicte
Gilman, Mark Greenberg, Beatrice Hohenegger, Anita Keys,
Kenneth Lapatin, Catherine Lorenz, Ann Lucke, Robin Ray,
Ellen M. Rosenbery, Lisa Talbot, and Maria Teresa Train for
their contribution to the book's accomplishment.
                    —Patrick Bowe

This book was enhanced immeasurably by the insight,
research, and dedication of the late landscape architect
Denis L. Kurutz. His original design and continued input
enabled the Villa Gardens to mature into the elegant
collection of Roman plants and trees we enjoy today.
                    —Michael D. DeHart

FRONT COVER: Front cover: *Punica granatum* (Outer
              Peristyle Garden)
BACK COVER: clockwise from left: *Cyclamen hederifolium*
              (East Garden); *Origanum dictamnus* (Herb
              Garden); *Citrus limon* (Herb Garden);
              Nymphaea sp. (Entry Path)
PAGE 1:   *Vitis vinifera* 'Perlette' (Outer Peristyle Garden)
PAGE 2:   Reflection (Inner Peristyle Garden)
PAGE 6:   *Erysimum cheiri* (*Cheiranthus cheiri*) (Outer
              Peristyle Garden)
PAGES 8–9:   Northeast View of the Villa Gardens
PAGES 30–31: *Anemone coronaria* (Outer Peristyle Garden)
PAGE 32:   *Scilla peruviana* (East Garden)
PAGE 153:   *Verbascum bombyciferum* 'Arctic Summer'
              (Herb Garden)
PAGE 160:   *Borago officinalis* (Herb Garden)

CONTENTS

FOREWORD   7

THE ROMAN GARDEN AND THE GETTY VILLA GARDENS

INTRODUCTION TO THE ROMAN GARDEN   11

THE GARDENS OF THE GETTY VILLA   23

THE GARDENS AND THEIR PLANTS

NOTE TO THE READER   33

MAP OF THE VILLA GARDENS   35

THE ENTRY PATH   57
THE INNER PERISTYLE GARDEN   59
THE EAST GARDEN   69
THE OUTER PERISTYLE GARDEN   83
THE HERB GARDEN   111

INDEX   153

When J. Paul Getty decided to model his new museum in California on an ancient Roman villa, he chose the Villa dei Papiri at Herculaneum with its extensive gardens. Mr. Getty's intention was for visitors to his villa to enjoy the pleasures of its gardens in addition to those of its collections; this was a novel idea at the time, but he realized that the mild Californian climate would allow a close interplay between internal and external spaces. The Getty Villa opened in 1974, and as a result of Mr. Getty's vision, visitors were offered a unique chance to experience a Roman villa and its gardens as they would have existed in antiquity.

We are grateful to renowned garden historian Patrick Bowe for his lively and informative essays exploring the design and uses of ancient Roman gardens as related to the planning of those at the Getty Villa. He describes the underlying concepts for each of the five gardens as well as their architectural and sculptural elements and their relationship to Roman models. During the more recent renovation, the Villa underwent vital conservation work, while the gardens' plantings were also updated as a result of a research trip to ancient sites in Europe. In the second part of the book, horticulturist Michael DeHart (Supervisor for Grounds and Gardens for the J. Paul Getty Trust) presents an extensive list of the latest plantings based on that research, describing growing habits, characteristics, and historical uses. All the essays and the plant descriptions are beautifully illustrated by Getty photographers Ellen Rosenbery, Tahnee Cracchiola, and Lisa Talbot.

We are confident that this handsome and long-awaited book, which is the companion volume to *Plants in the Getty's Central Garden*, will be a fascinating guide for visitors to the Getty Villa gardens and for readers interested in Roman plant history.

David Bomford
Acting Director, The J. Paul Getty Museum

INTRODUCTION TO THE ROMAN GARDEN

The gardens of the Getty Villa are based on those of the Villa dei Papiri (Villa of the Papyri), an ancient Roman residence that was located at Herculaneum on the Bay of Naples, Italy. Like the rest of the ancient city, the villa was buried by pyroclastic flow and volcanic mud during the eruption of Mount Vesuvius in A.D. 79. The following chapter will look at this villa in some detail, but first it is useful to sketch what is known about the Roman garden generally.

A typical Roman villa was planned around a central atrium open to the sky. Rainwater fell through an opening in the roof (*compluvium*) and was collected in a central pool (*impluvium*), whence it flowed through a drain to an underground storage tank. The water could then be drawn from the tank for use during the dry summer season. Some villas, however, were connected to local water systems, fed by aqueducts, and thus could rely on a constant source of fresh water to feed fountains, pools, and other aquatic features. Because the area of the atrium surrounding the *impluvium* was roofed, people could walk in the open air from one part of the house to another while still being protected from the summer sun or the winter rainfall. Many Roman houses and most villas also had courtyards surrounded by colonnades called peristyles, and gardens, too, were often surrounded by columns. These could be used for exercise, such as running or walking, and are called peristyle gardens. Although most Roman villas faced onto a peristyle garden and were therefore inward looking, some villas looked outward to take advantage of views over the sea or the countryside.

The Roman garden reflected in its design the architectural lines of the house or villa to which it was attached. For example, vistas in a garden were designed as a continuation of vistas within or through the house, and the form and proportion of a garden's spaces echoed those of the home's interior. Gardens were usually formal in design, being laid out along straight or geometrically curved lines. They were also usually laid out in strict bilateral symmetry around a central axis. Thus, a tree or statue situated on one side of a central axis would be matched by another on the opposite side.

The gardens of large Roman villas often had a number of diverse spaces and uses. One section of a garden might have been used for recreation and leisure, another for health and exercise, and yet another for utilitarian purposes, such as food production. Gardens were also viewed as settings in which works of art might be displayed. Antique Greek and contemporary Roman statuary was set out along a garden's walkways or terraces and positioned in its courtyards or inside garden pavilions.

The grandest villa gardens were notable for their extensive exercise facilities such as baths, gymnasiums, stadiums, and hippodromes, though these, being private, were on a smaller scale than those in cities for public use. Walking exercise was often a group activity, during which participants conversed or read aloud. Pliny the Younger (*Letters* 2.17) noted that the pleasure of walking in the gymnasium of his villa at Laurentum was enhanced by the scent of the garden's violets.

Some garden areas were devoted to food production. Excavations in the gardens of villas at Boscoreale, north of Pompeii, have revealed extensive raised beds for growing vegetables. A circular wellhead was also found; it covered a deep cistern, from which stored water was drawn to irrigate the garden. At first, only a limited range of vegetables and fruits was grown, but as the geographical boundaries of the Empire expanded, many new plants were introduced to the Roman garden. Some came from conquered territories, but others were brought as a result of the increased trade with neighboring regions. Newly discovered fruits and vegetables were imported from far-flung areas, acclimatized, and then planted in Roman gardens.

In general, Roman gardens were characterized by a balance between their increasingly diverse plantings and their rich architectural and sculptural decoration in the form of arbors, pergolas, trelliswork, fountains, and statuary.

Arbors and pergolas are open structures that provide overhead shade to areas in a garden. In the Roman garden, arbors were usually room-like structures used for sedentary activities like sitting or dining. The *pergula*—Latin for "projecting eave"—usually described a structure that provided shade for more-active pursuits, say, walking along a garden's pathways. Some ancient Roman arbors and pergolas were constructed largely of stone or marble. Pliny the Younger (*Letters* 5.6) describes a dining table in his garden that was shaded by a trelliswork arbor supported by four matching columns of white marble. In a typical pergola construction, simple pillars of stone, or in some cases brick or less-permanent materials such as wood, supported a light overhead lattice of timber, which provided dappled shade underneath. Climbing plants such as grapevines, roses, and gourds were trained up and over the latticework to provide increased shade as required. Because they were built wholly or in part out of light, perishable materials, no arbors or pergolas have survived in their entirety from antiquity. However, examples depicted in mural paintings, such as one from the Villa of Publius Fannius Synistor at Boscoreale, now in the Metropolitan Museum of Art in New York, enable us to imagine how they looked.

Large Roman gardens were often divided into smaller subsidiary spaces by trellises—or latticework screens and fences. These provided strong visual delineation between different areas but, being perforated, also allowed the free movement of cooling breezes from one area of the garden to the next. Such freedom of air movement was important during the hot summers typical of southern Italy. Because of the perishable nature of wood, only fragments of latticework have been found in excavations. However, mural paintings show a variety of designs. One such painting, from an unidentified villa near Pompeii, now in the National Archaeological Museum of Naples, shows the construction of latticework arches, bowers, fences, and ornamental urns, all unified in one integrated overall design.

A number of Roman gardens were adorned with nymphaea, or artificial grottoes. The word "nymphaeum" was first used in the Graeco-Roman world to refer to a natural cave inhabited by nymphs: semidivine females associated with aspects of nature. People in antiquity are known to have frequented natural caves, which no doubt offered a cool respite from the summer heat. Thousands of knucklebones, used for divination and games of chance in the ancient world, have been found in the Corycian Cave on the slopes of Mount Parnassus in Greece, suggesting that it was

used as a place of retreat and ritual. Romans strove to replicate this shady atmosphere in their gardens by constructing artificial caves, also referred to as nymphaea, which were sometimes little more than niches in a wall. The Romans deliberately chose rough stones such as pumice and lava stone or rough-cut stones such as cleft travertine for their garden nymphaea, so as to echo the uneven surfaces of natural caves. The interiors of garden nymphaea were faced with unusual stones as well as seashells and colorful pieces of vitreous material in a geological decorative scheme. Because many natural caves are fed by springs, water—in the form of a fountain or cascade—was also introduced into nymphaca. A trickle of water might be designed to fall from an outlet in the wall and then cascade down a flight of marble steps into a pool, as in the House of the Great Fountain in Pompeii.

Water occupied a special place in the Roman garden. Pools varied in size from small basins found in townhouse courtyards to the large sheets of ornamental water associated with aristocratic or imperial residences. Excavations have revealed pools at a number of ancient residences, including the aristocratic Villa San Marco at Stabiae and the larger imperial villa of Hadrian at Tivoli near Rome. Such pools varied in the complexity of their design from the simplest geometric shapes to complex groups of interlocking forms, sometimes on different levels and linked to each other by cascades. Excavated examples can be seen in the House of Loreius Tiburtinus at Pompeii and in the House of the Water jets in Conimbriga, Portugal. Some pools were simple bathing pools, while others were used as fishponds. The latter usually had shady subsurface alcoves into which fish could retreat to breed or to avoid the hot summer sun.

Pools were usually made of concrete while the associated pipework was of wood or lead. The inner surfaces of some Pompeian pools were painted blue, perhaps to imitate the color of the Mediterranean. Other pools were lined with tile, also often in blue, whereas luxury pools might be lined with marble or dressed stone. Yet other pools were painted with scenes of marine life, which would then appear to be swimming in the water.

Fountains are frequently illustrated in paintings of Roman gardens. The water for garden fountains was transported by gravity flow from nearby springs, streams, or specially constructed storage tanks. Water from a public aqueduct might also be available but was expensive to purchase. Fountains thus became symbols of a garden owner's wealth, not to say extravagance, although the overflow water from fountains rarely went to waste: from the fountain pools it was channelled to irrigate the owner's gardens and orchards. In early Roman times, technology was such that only very modest jets of water rose from the fountains. These must nonetheless have been attractive, as even a low fountain jet could evoke the bubbling of a natural spring. Later advances in hydraulic technology allowed for more-elaborate garden fountains with higher jets and often incorporated statuary. Among the figures favored for these sculptures were gods and goddesses associated with the sea, nymphs, fauns, children, and dolphins.

The most frequently illustrated type of Roman fountain is one with a low jet of water bubbling up from a stone or marble bowl mounted on a pedestal. The bowls usually had broad carved brims and were sometimes fluted on the exterior. The bowls' pedestals also varied in design, some being fluted and others given carved stone handles. A fountain bowl illustrated in a wall painting in the so-called Villa of Poppaea at Oplontis has an elaborate pedestal in the form of a kneeling winged figure, which appears to be sculpted in stone.

Statuary played an important part in the decoration of Roman gardens. Sculptures—often depicting mythological subjects, notable athletes, politicians, or philosophers—were intended to inspire thoughtful reflection as a visitor walked through a garden. The careful choice of a particular god, ancient philosopher, nymph, or animal might establish a specific garden atmosphere or theme. Figurative sculpture of this kind was usually life-size and set on a pedestal or base for greater visibility. It was sometimes painted in realistic colors or might be gilded to give a richer, more luxurious effect. In some gardens, statuary seems to have been placed at random, while in others the arrangement followed an organized scheme or symbolic program. Often the pieces were placed in a direct relationship with the architectural features of a building, for example, between the columns of a portico or colonnade.

The preferred subjects of fountain statuary, as mentioned above, were those associated with water, such as sea-gods or marine creatures. Fountain statuary was often made of bronze rather than stone because the hollow center of a bronze figure could conceal the fountain's pipework.

Certain forms of statuary—herms, *pinakes*, and *oscilli*—had a special association with the Roman garden. Herms were statues with a head or bust mounted on top of a stone shaft or marble pillar. Both the term and the form were derived from images of the Greek god Hermes, which were thought to confer luck and fertility. Later they were used for images of other gods, mythological figures, and even portraits. A *pinax* (pl. *pinakes*, from the Greek word for "board") was a decorative panel painted or carved in low relief, representing a mythological figure or scene. It might also be raised on a stone shaft for better viewing. An *oscillum* (small mask) was a disc, also carved in low relief, which was hung by a chain from the architrave or ceiling of a portico to oscillate in wind.

Romans used plant forms and colors to complement and enhance the architectural and sculptural ornament in their gardens. They made extensive use of native evergreen trees and shrubs: stone pine, bay laurel, laurustinus (*Viburnum tinus*), strawberry tree, common myrtle, European box, and common ivy. These formed a sober, year-round foliage background to the bright colors of the many flowering shrubs, perennials, and annuals. As noted above, the Romans also used plant species that had been introduced from countries they interacted with through conquest or trade. Planting is ephemeral, and no examples of living gardens survive from the Roman period. However, in recent decades, research at Pompeii carried out by the botanical archaeologist Wilhelmina Jashemski has enabled us to identify, from the shape and size of root cavities preserved in the volcanic ash, some of the woody plants grown in these gardens. This, and later research by Maureen

Carroll at Pompeii and Kathryn Gleason at Stabiae and elsewhere, has also enabled us to identify the precise locations of certain species in the gardens where they were planted.

Surviving mural paintings also offer a guide as to the arrangement of plants within a Roman garden. These paintings usually illustrate layered or tiered planting schemes in which small plants are used in the front section of a bed, larger shrubs behind, while taller trees are positioned to form a background to the whole planting. Wall paintings also show that plantings were sometimes punctuated visually at rhythmic intervals by prominent individual trees such as oriental planes. Although these paintings depict very dense plantings, archaeological evidence indicates that garden plants were, in fact, more widely spaced than the paintings would suggest. It is important to note in this context that such wall paintings did not necessarily depict reality but may rather have been intended to represent an ideal world, giving the impression of a fecund, paradisiacal setting.

A number of plants were grown for use in making the garlands, wreaths, and crowns that were worn during Roman celebrations and festivities. Certain plants would have been grown by devotees of a cult for their customary association with a given deity: the bay laurel sacred to Apollo, the olive tree to Minerva, and so forth.

In the hot Mediterranean climate, a primary task of the gardener was the creation of shade. So numerous were the tree- and vine-shaded courtyards in Pompeii that an observer looking down from above would have seen a "green" city. Excavations at Pompeii have revealed a variety of planting schemes for trees: in some garden courts, the trees appear to have been planted at random, while in others, a more formal scheme is at work, with trees planted in the center and/or at each corner of the court.

The oriental plane tree, imported to Rome from Greece, was possibly the most widely used tree for shade planting. It is a highly adaptable species, tolerating pruning to whatever size or shape its allotted space requires without loss of vigor, hence it was and continues to be especially common in built-up areas. Its large leaves are supported on long, flexible stems, so they sway even in the slightest breath of wind, creating a cooling draft in the tree's vicinity. Date palms, imported from the Near East, are frequently depicted in garden mural paintings as well. Their long, feather-like arrangement of leaf blades would have rustled attractively in the wind, though the trees did not bear ripe dates in the Italian climate, which is cooler than that of their native range.

Fruit trees were selected to shade smaller courtyards and gardens as well as to provide an edible crop in season. In the so-called Villa of Poppaea at Oplontis, for example, the remains of a double row of citron trees were found during a garden excavation, each tree planted in line with one of the columns of the villa's portico.

In Roman wall paintings, the most commonly depicted garden shrubs are the native ever-greens such as common laurel, bay laurel, common myrtle, oleander, and laurustinus. Shrubs that are noted primarily for their attractive flowering are less commonly depicted.

A number of species and varieties of roses were grown. Among those known to us from literary sources are the Rose of Paestum, named for the ancient city south of present-day Naples; the Rose of Praeneste (modern Palestrina), near Rome, which was prized as a late-flowering variety; and the Rose of Cyrene, about which we know only that it was native to that ancient city in what is now Libya. Also grown were two native wild rose species whose descriptions correspond to roses we know today as the damask rose and the cabbage rose. The latter was possibly the "cabbage-type" or centifolia rose to which Pliny the Elder referred (*Natural History* 21.10).

In addition to the roses, several dwarf shrubs were used for ornamental landscaping. Among these, the evergreen butcher's broom and rosemary, the latter especially suited to seaside gardens, seem to have been prominent.

By today's standards, the variety of trees and shrubs available to a gardener in ancient Rome was limited. Therefore, creating topiaries added to the range of interesting forms that might be seen in a garden. Pliny the Younger (*Letters* 5.6) described topiaries in a variety of predetermined

geometric or representational shapes such as obelisks or pyramids. Pliny the Elder (*Natural History* 16.60) wrote of complex topiaries in which groups of plants were trimmed to represent entire hunting scenes or a fleet of ships. Topiaries are, and must have been then, especially attractive to owners of small or city gardens because trees and shrubs that are naturally large can be kept within bounds by regular clipping. Straightforward clipped hedges, both of cypress and of boxwood, were also used, customarily, as boundaries and space dividers. Pliny the Younger (*Letters* 5.6) described seeing boxwood hedges that were clipped in tiers.

Vines and other climbing plants were also popular in ancient Roman gardens because when grown over arbors, pergolas, and trellis screens, they contributed to a garden's shade. The grapevine, morning glory, common ivy, and common smilax were most frequently used for this purpose. Vines were also used ornamentally, at times trained along ropes loosely suspended between columns or trees so as to produce decorative swags of foliage and fruit.

Although trees and shrubs predominated in Roman gardens, flowers, particularly native species, were also common. The Madonna lily, martagon lily, wild chrysanthemum, corn poppy, and periwinkle are all depicted in garden mural paintings. In addition, iris, cistus, and the common daisy are depicted in the surviving murals of the House of Livia at Prima Porta near Rome. Literary sources indicate the cultivation of other flowers such as acanthus, violet, narcissus, hyacinth, hound's tongue, forget-me-not, common kidney vetch, and common vervain. Archaeological excavations in garden soils at Pompeii and neighboring sites have yielded seeds of yet more flowers, including asters, pinks, mallows, campanulas, lychnis, chickweed, and plantains. It is reasonable to assume that many native bulbs such as narcissus, crocus, gladiolus, squill, and members of the ornamental onion family were domesticated and grown in gardens, although the narcissus is the only one shown in garden paintings. At least two fern species—the hart's tongue and the maidenhair—appear to have been grown as ornamental plants. A rich palette of floral color and form was undoubtedly available to the ancient Roman gardener.

Fruit trees such as fig, citron, quince, pomegranate, and both golden and purple plums are depicted in Roman garden murals. In addition, the cultivation of apple, cornel, medlar, mulberry, serviceberry, crabapple, and carob trees is recorded in literary sources. The Romans also experimented with tree species that had been imported from abroad. A fresco from the House of the Orchard, Pompeii, shows cultivated lemons, and we know that oranges, like the lemons native to East Asia, fruited in some imperial gardens. Other examples of exotic tree fruit growing in Roman gardens included the cherry, imported from the Pontic region of present-day Turkey; the apricot, from Armenia; the peach and the damson plum, from Syria; and the pomegranate and the jujube, from North Africa. Unusual varieties of common fruits were also imported for cultivation: a "round" apple variety from western Greece, a "Syrian red" variety, and one brought from present-day Belgium. Nut trees such as almond, walnut, and sweet chestnut must also have been grown, since there is evidence that the Romans introduced them to Britain. The Roman agricultural writer Palladius recommends the now unusual practice of planting pomegranates in large terracotta pots, and Pliny the Elder suggests that lemon trees might be grown in pots, a practice that continues in gardens today. In addition to the many kinds of tree fruits, bush fruits such as raspberry, blackberry, and strawberry were also cultivated.

The production of vegetables in kitchen gardens was already a highly developed skill in Roman times. Pliny the Elder (*Natural History* 19.24–27) notes that gourd, turnip, radish, and parsnip, among other vegetables, were grown, while Cato the Elder, author of a famed treatise on agriculture, refers to various members of the cabbage family (*De agricultura* 156). He also mentions the cultivation of asparagus. Since it is known that the Romans introduced them to cultivation in Britain, it is evident that celery, coriander, cucumber, dill, garlic, onion, orache (a spinach-like green), parsley, radish, and turnip were also grown. Some plants were grown for multiple uses. Plants like thyme and mint were employed for flavoring but were also specially grown by beekeepers for the production of aromatic honey. Mustard, used in cooking, was also known as a cure for a number of health complaints.

The gardens of ancient Rome were diverse in size and design and in their uses. Their symmetrical forms—punctuated with pavilions, grottoes, statuary, pools, and fountains—clearly appealed to J. Paul Getty (1892–1976), the Museum's founder. As we shall see in the following chapter, his keen interest in the ephemeral art of the garden is an essential part of his legacy.

THE GARDENS OF THE GETTY VILLA

In 1912, at the age of nineteen, J. Paul Getty visited the excavated cities of Pompeii and Herculaneum, which had been destroyed in the eruption of Mount Vesuvius in A.D. 79. He also visited the National Archaeological Museum in Naples, where many of the artworks excavated from these ancient cities are on display. He was so impressed by what he saw that Greek and Roman antiquities became a lifelong interest and, eventually, a focus of his art acquisition. Nearly sixty years later, when Mr. Getty decided to build a museum in California to house his art collection, he elected to base its design on that of an ancient Roman villa. He believed such a building would provide an appropriate environment for the display of his antiquities and would allow museum visitors to feel a sense of continuity with the past. It would also provide an intimate, domestic setting for the works of art, in welcome contrast to the intimidating, impersonal scale that is characteristic of many of the world's institutional museums. His vision was to prove immensely popular with visitors to the Villa, which opened in 1974. The museum has also found a place in the specialized literature of scholars of Roman villas as a contemporary exercise in archaeological reconstruction.

Villas in ancient Rome were country houses and estates used by their owners as quiet, rural retreats, away from the noise and bustle of the city. As places of relaxation and entertainment, villas often included several beautiful gardens, richly decorated with sculpture. The villa on which Mr. Getty chose to base his new museum's design was the magnificent Villa dei Papiri (Villa of the Papyri), located just outside the city of Herculaneum on the Bay of Naples. This villa, like much of the surrounding area, was buried by volcanic debris, which had hardened to the consistency of cement. Collectors and students of antiquities in the eighteenth century had partially excavated the villa by tunneling through this debris. The villa's name derives from the hundreds of carbonized papyrus rolls found during these excavations.

A great many works of art were uncovered during the exploration of the villa. The Roman-era owner had displayed works of art not only in the interior rooms of his villa but also in its courtyards and gardens, and especially in association with the garden fountains. These works are now housed in the National Archaeological Museum in Naples.

For a variety of reasons, the excavations were halted, not to be resumed until the late twentieth century. But one of the chief excavators in the earlier age, Karl Weber (1712–1764), a Swiss army engineer, had taken copious notes and made a systematic (if partial) plan of the villa.

Careful examination of Weber's plan has suggested to some scholars that the Villa dei Papiri and its gardens were not laid out all at once but rather evolved over several centuries. It is thought that the original villa consisted of a relatively simple house constructed around an atrium or courtyard and that, probably in the first century B.C., a second extensive courtyard may have been added, forming a garden with a large central pool surrounded by a covered colonnade. This and other pools and fountains in the villa's gardens would have required a steady and plentiful supply of water, and Weber reported that during his investigations he found a complex, subterranean hydraulic system.

Mr. Getty was attracted to Weber's plan as a basis for planning his new museum. The Villa dei Papiri is thought to have belonged to an important historical figure, Lucius Calpurnius Piso, Julius Caesar's father-in-law, who was consul of Rome in 58 B.C. Like Getty himself, the owner had assembled a major collection of art. The sixty-four-acre property in the Cañon de Sentimiento at Malibu that Mr. Getty had purchased in 1945 lies in a suburb close to the sea, as did the Villa dei Papiri. Additionally, the Malibu property lies at approximately the same latitude as the Bay of Naples and has a similarly mild, semi-arid climate. Most importantly, the plan of the Villa dei Papiri suggested that it may have had extensive gardens. This fact was of special interest to Mr. Getty, who regarded gardens as an important part of his museum project.

Gardens had long held a special meaning to Mr. Getty. It is noteworthy that the principal character in the novella *A Journey from Corinth*, set in ancient Greece and Italy, which Getty wrote and published in 1955, was a landscape architect. In the novella, Getty even describes the putative owner of the Villa dei Papiri, Calpurnius Piso, as being "more concerned with directing building and in laying out gardens . . . than in collecting statues and paintings." Getty's keen interest in the development of the Villa's gardens was fully shared by Stephen Garrett, his architectural advisor and the museum's first director.

The planners of the new museum realized that the mild climate of Southern California would allow a close interplay between the exterior and interior spaces of the complex, that is, between galleries and gardens. If the display spaces were planned carefully, sunlight and the sound of the gardens' fountains, and even occasional light breezes, might pervade some of the museum's galleries. It was envisioned from the outset that visitors to the Villa would be able to explore the gardens, should "art fatigue" set in. It was even foreseen that certain visitors might be attracted to the museum solely for its gardens.

Recent excavations in Herculaneum have revealed that the Villa dei Papiri had at least three stories. This information was not available to Weber, however, and his plan, upon which the Getty Villa is based, provided an outline of one level only. Although many of the statues from the gardens—at least eighty-five individual pieces—have been unearthed and a number of papyrus scrolls have now been opened and read, little of the fine detail that would have been needed for an accurate reconstruction of the villa's architecture and gardens was available to Mr. Getty's designers. To create a detailed design for both the Getty Villa and the gardens, Mr. Getty and his historical consultant—the archaeologist Norman Neuerburg—were therefore obliged to assemble information derived from other villas and gardens of the period that had been more fully excavated. The Roman gardens of Pompeii, Herculaneum, and the nearby town of Stabiae were studied in detail. Paintings of gardens that remained on the walls of some ancient houses in Pompeii, Herculaneum, and Rome, especially a painting from the House of Livia in Prima Porta, were also carefully examined. Writings by ancient authors on gardens, plants, and agriculture, such as Pliny the Elder, Varro, and Dioscorides, were consulted. In addition, the plantings in the gardens have been renewed in the light of more recent knowledge derived from a new source: the analysis of carbonized roots, seeds, fruits, vegetables, nuts, and woods found in scientific excavations in Pompeii and elsewhere by Dr. Jashemski and her colleagues.

In the creation of the new museum gardens, compromises had to be made between architectural and horticultural fidelity to the plan of the Villa dei Papiri and contemporary functional demands. The building and its gardens had to conform to the canyon topography of the Malibu site as well as to modern building codes; to the practical needs of a garden open to the public, including security requirements; and to the amenities expected by visitors. Physical conditions imposed certain constraints. The soil in Malibu differs from the volcanic soil of Herculaneum. The incidence of fog in Malibu is greater than that in the Bay of Naples, which affected the choice of plantings: an Asian boxwood rather than English boxwood was selected for the garden's dwarf hedges, for example. In fact, when the fog rolls in from the ocean, the Getty Villa and its canyon take on a dreamlike atmosphere unlike anything one experiences in southern Italy. Although copies of the statuary excavated from the Villa dei Papiri were placed in the gardens, it was not always possible to locate them in conformity with the original findspots. In fact, the new gardens had to be a creative and functional adaptation of the ancient horticultural design, a reinterpretation of the original gardens rather than a replica of them, an evocation rather than an imitation.

To assist him in the achievement of his gardens, Mr. Getty hired a firm of landscape architects, Emmet Wemple and Associates, but he kept a close eye on their work to make sure their ideas were in keeping with his own. In his novella, Mr. Getty seems to have been voicing his own views when he has Calpurnius Piso say to his new landscape architect, "If you understand that I mean to have my own way in landscaping, and you wish to act as my assistant and further my efforts, instead of trying to thwart them, you and I should get along very well."

The gardens of the Getty Villa are composed of a series of linked individual spaces. They are characterized by a rich combination of architecture, plantings, fountains, and statuary, and each

is arranged in strict bilateral symmetry around a central axis, as were the gardens of the luxury villas of ancient Rome. The gardens reflect the Villa's architecture in their size and scale. The Inner Peristyle Garden, for example, echoes the layout and rhythm of its surrounding colonnade. The width of the Outer Peristyle Garden is related closely to the width of the building. The dimensions of the East and Herb gardens also correspond to the dimensions of the building. The gardens' plantings, too, reflect this close relationship: for example, the rhythm of the lines of laurel trees in the Outer Peristyle Garden reflects the rhythm of the colonnade columns behind.

The range of plants available to the Roman gardener was more limited than that available to gardeners today. The highly developed, showy forms of many contemporary garden plants were not seen in the ancient Roman garden. In order to create an authentic atmosphere, the Getty Villa gardens rarely use such modern plant varieties. For example, the only oleanders planted are of the original variety—in a single shade of pink—rather than any of the more colorful modern varieties.

Because many of the plants used in the Roman garden have a short flowering season, the Villa gardens rely for their sustained, year-round color mostly on foliage evergreens. These plants yield an interesting variety of effects by the many different ways in which they are grown. Many of the trees and shrubs are "topiarized" or trained in such a way as to produce a specific form or shape. Laurel trees, which form the foundation planting of some of the gardens, are trimmed three times a year so that they do not outgrow their predetermined shapes and sizes.

Geometrically trimmed dwarf hedges, in a variety of evergreen plant materials such as rosemary, butcher's broom, and boxwood, define many of the garden beds. For example, approximately 3,500 plants are required to provide the nearly one mile of box hedging that is used throughout the Outer Peristyle Garden. Maintaining the hedging and the various topiaries is costly and demanding, as gardeners must carefully trim the plants to the correct shape and size on each occasion. Other plants also demand careful maintenance, such as the ivies that are trained over dome-shaped wire frames to produce low mounds of foliage. Grapevines are trained to grow up through latticework and over arbors and must be cut back on a regular basis.

In the initial stages of the planting, large specimens of bay laurel, European fan palm, stone pine, and pomegranate were purchased to give a mature look to the garden. Although some seeds and bulbs initially had to be imported from Italy, and the boxwood was sourced in Northern California and Oregon, all of the garden's plantings are now sourced in Southern California. In spring, 6,500 crocuses, 1,000 grape hyacinths, and 1,000 narcissi and other spring bulbs provide the garden with abundant color. Perennials such as bellflowers, irises, and lilies succeed the bulbs with their cool, Mediterranean summer floral color. Redwood headers are sunk in the soil to mark distinct planting areas within each bed, with one area for perennials and annuals and another for flowering bulbs that resent disturbance. Mats of ground-covering plants are developed to fill the spaces between the trees and shrubs. Where the ground is not covered with plants, the sandy soil is carefully raked to provide a neat finish.

The pools, fountains, statuary, and other artifacts function as additional garden elements and contribute to the overall effect. Water provides the central focus in each constituent garden at the Villa, though in each garden it has a different character. In the Inner Peristyle Garden, the central water feature is a narrow, shallow marble pool, while in the East Garden, it is a fountain raised on a pedestal, its splashing water animating the surrounding space. In the Outer Peristyle Garden, water forms a broad, placid mirror to the sky. The Herb Garden has a formal dipping pool, of the kind used in Roman gardens to provide water to the plants in the surrounding beds.

In addition to the water features, the bronze statuary acts as a foil to the gardens' vegetation. All of the pieces are cast from molds taken from statuary found in the Villa dei Papiri, now in the National Archaeological Museum in Naples. In the nineteenth century, the Chiurazzi Artistic Foundry (Fonderia Artistica Chiurazzi)—established in 1840 in Naples by Gennaro Chiurazzi—received permission to make molds for the reproduction of the antique sculptures from the Villa dei Papiri. The foundry, now operating under the name of Fonderia Storica Chiurazzi, still has these historic molds, and in the 1970s Mr. Getty was able to order copies of the original statuary for his gardens.

The collection includes many impressive, life-size, full-length sculptures of gods, demigods, human figures, and animals. It also includes twenty-four life-size bronze busts representing gods, heroes, and sages of ancient Greece and Rome, all set on white Carrara marble pedestals. To the extent possible, the statuary is placed in spots corresponding to where Weber found the originals in the gardens of the Villa dei Papiri. Their presence in the Villa gardens today inspires visitors to imagine and reflect on the art, religion, and history of ancient Rome.

While many small-scale structures and artifacts in the Villa gardens are designed to underscore their ancient Roman character, it would have been impractical, given the anticipated pedestrian traffic, to surface the gardens' main paths with loose gravel, as would have been done in ancient Rome. Instead, decorative forms of gravel have been set in cement to give what is called "an exposed aggregate finish," thus simulating a traditional gravel path with something more robust. However, loose sand or gravel is used to surface the gardens' subsidiary paths where there is less foot traffic.

The gardens' handsome light fixtures are based on the lanterns that the Romans carried through their unlit streets at night. Made of bronze, and fitted with alabaster or imitation alabaster rather than glass, these fixtures, used during occasional evening events at the Villa, emit a warm glow that evokes the olive-oil lamps used in ancient times. The paint color selected for the gardens' many concrete benches, planters, and lantern pedestals is, appropriately, Pompeian red; the gardens' benches are discreetly inset in beds and borders so as not to stand out unduly in the overall garden picture.

From a technical point of view, the Inner and Outer Peristyle gardens, because they are located over the parking structure and other below-grade facilities, require special soil mixtures, as well as special care in planting and maintenance. The demands of maintenance are eased by the fact that all the gardens at the Villa boast an unobtrusive subsurface irrigation system at two levels. This ensures that both plants with shallow root systems and those with deeper ones get their appropriate water.

The gardens of the Getty Villa provide an opportunity for the visitor to experience the ancient Roman garden, which was an important forerunner of later Western gardens. Mr. Getty never saw the completed gardens, because after 1960 he rarely ventured far from his English home, Sutton Place. Like the Roman emperor Hadrian, whom he quotes in his novella, Getty "had come to a time in life when the inconveniences of ancient travel made him loath to take long journeys." Although he never visited the Villa, he kept in close touch with its development, and especially with the development of its gardens, by means of constant reports, large-scale photo boards, and even films. He commented with satisfaction after the gardens were completed in 1974, "I believe that the ancient Roman proprietor of the Villa dei Papiri would find the peristyle garden in the Museum very close to the one in Herculaneum."

NOTE TO THE READER

MICROCLIMATE

The conditions described in this book are reflective of the microclimate in the coastal canyon environment found at the Getty Villa. Other conditions away from the coast will require differing water needs and protection from temperature extremes. Local nurseries can provide advice on specific area conditions.

WATERING

A great deal of the plants at the Villa are drought tolerant, which is why the following plant descriptions rarely have watering instructions. In general, the answer to the question of how often to water will vary by circumstance. Sites and soils vary; sun and shade change with the seasons. Check soil for moisture by digging down a few inches. A soil probe is a great investment, as the surface condition rarely tells you what is happening at root level.

Roots seek out moisture and resist growing into dry areas. They will also drown if kept too wet. So spend some time learning about the soil in your garden.

New plantings need more frequent irrigation to become established. Keep the root mass moist to start; pretend it is still in a pot by building a small dam around the root ball and directing water to it. As the roots grow out and become established, you can reduce the frequency of watering.

FERTILIZING

Ancient Romans applied fish as a fertilizer when planting new plants. Modern fertilizers are used at the Villa to enhance plant health. Organic sources are used whenever possible; however, many Mediterranean plants thrive best in poor soils and thus do not require added fertilizer.

FLOWERING TIMES

Bloom periods are given for coastal Southern California.

TEMPERATURES

All temperatures are given in Fahrenheit.

DISCLAIMER

The information included in the following plant descriptions is not intended as a guide to self-medication. Readers interested in the medicinal use of plants should discuss the topic with a doctor, pharmacist, nurse, or other authorized health-care provider. Neither the authors nor the J. Paul Getty Trust accepts responsibility for the accuracy of the pharmacological information itself or for the consequences of any use or misuse of the information in this book.

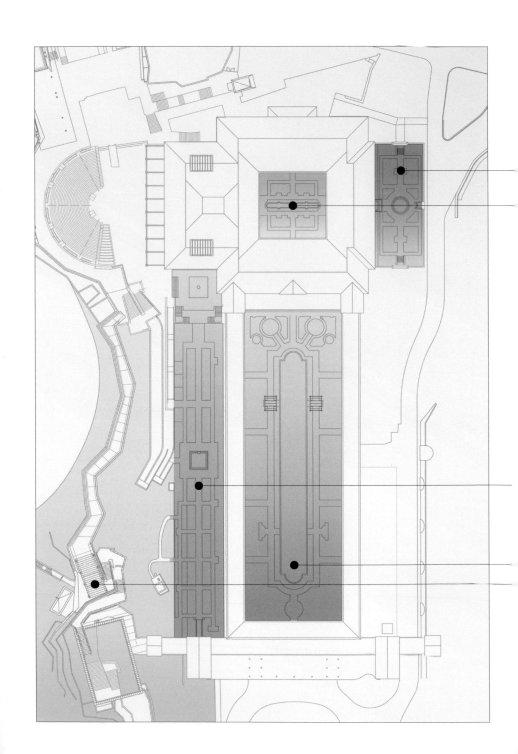

MAP OF THE VILLA GARDENS

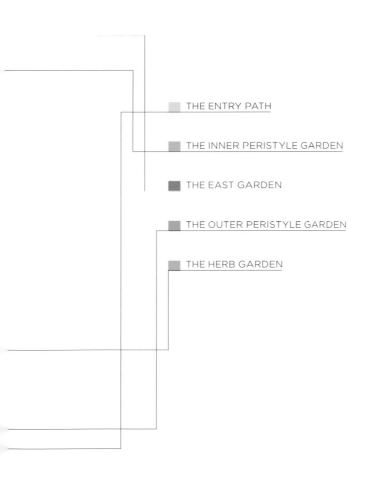

THE ENTRY PATH

THE INNER PERISTYLE GARDEN

THE EAST GARDEN

THE OUTER PERISTYLE GARDEN

THE HERB GARDEN

The entrance driveway to the sixty-four-acre site of the Getty Villa leaves the Pacific Coast Highway through double-arched entrance gates and enters a steep sided wooded canyon, the Cañon de Sentimiento. Alongside the driveway, a spring feeds a rock-strewn stream and pools, decorated with ornamental aquatic and marginal plants, all growing in the dappled shade of mature specimens of native California sycamore and coast redwood. The driveway is surfaced with bomanite, a patented material, patterned to resemble the irregular, large-block paving that was used in streets and roads throughout the Roman Empire.

Eventually, the driveway reaches the entry façade of the Villa, which stretches like a bridge across the narrow canyon. Behind its ground-level arches lies the original parking garage, which is still in use today. To the left of the driveway, a new multi-story car park is veiled in vegetation in order to preserve as much as possible of the wooded integrity of the canyon. Its roof is planted with shrubs such as oleander and Jerusalem sage, screening the structure from above. In summer, English daisy, California poppy, marigold, and white yarrow seed themselves in large colonies between the shrubs to form a rooftop wildflower meadow. Extensive planters, running along the length of the building at each level, are filled with plants such as prostrate rosemary and Moroccan bindweed that hang down vertically and clad the structure's walls in greenery.

Nearby, the Entry Pavilion to the Villa takes the form of a roofless "room" that is partially buried in the sidewall of the canyon. The pavilion dates from the museum's reconstruction in the early twenty-first century and contains a range of visitor services. It creates a tunnel-like entrance that acts as a valve between the outside world and the inner "world" of the museum and its grounds. From the Entry Pavilion, stairs and elevators bring the visitor up to a high-level Entry Path, or raised walkway, cut into the upper flank of the wooded canyon. The elevation of the walkway ensures that a visitor benefits from the gentle, refreshing breezes that blow off the ocean. From here, the visitor can enjoy a first view back over the Pacific and, in another direction, glimpse the Getty Villa for the first time from above. This is a deliberate echo of the archaeological site at Herculaneum, where the visitor first sees the partially excavated Villa dei Papiri from

above, as the ground level at Herculaneum today is between 60 and 100 feet above what it was when the Villa dei Papiri was built.

Walking along the path, the visitor is introduced gradually to the Mediterranean world through terraced hillside gardens of trees, shrubs, and herbs that are native to that part of the world. Spire-like Italian cypresses; spreading Italian alders; European fan palms, with their clusters of dramatic fan-shaped leaves; as well as evergreen strawberry trees (so called because their fruits resemble strawberries) cluster in groups around the walkway. To these are added Canary Island pines and Italian stone pines, sometimes called umbrella pines on account of their umbrella-like canopy. The umbrella pines, characteristic of the Roman skyline, have been planted near the top of the canyon so that, in years to come, their broad canopies will dominate the horizon on the canyon's west side. When seen silhouetted against the sky, they will increase the impact of the Mediterranean flora in this part of the Villa's garden. The dark green leaves of young Mediterranean holm oaks strike a somber note, as does the foliage of the cork oak (in Portugal and Spain, the rugged bark of this tree is harvested to provide the material for wine-bottle corks). The pinkish red flowers of the Judas tree (*Cercis siliquastrum*), a small but delicately foliaged European relative of the American redbud, show brightly in early spring. The flowering smoke bushes, so called because their inflorescences are so fine that they resemble smoke when seen from a distance, bloom later in the year.

Smaller plants intervene. These include Pride of Madeira, with its elegant blue flower spikes; St. John's wort, its petals a rich yellow; Jerusalem sage, with a paler yellow flower of an unusual beaked shape; the carpeting periwinkle; acanthus, with its complex, shiny leaves; and the silver-leaved caryopteris. A matrix of olive trees in one area is underplanted with Italian meadow grasses. The olive trees are of a variety—developed by Swan Hill Nurseries—that is fruitless, thus avoiding the messy fruit drop that occurs with traditional fruiting olives.

Proceeding toward the Villa, it gradually becomes apparent that the retaining walls on either side of the high-level walkway, with their bands of stone and concrete, have been designed to evoke the stratified walls of an archaeological excavation. The materials used include wood-grained concrete, contrasting black marble, afrormosia wood, and both rough-cut and dressed travertine, a stone widely used in ancient Rome. The morning glories and Boston ivies, grown to partially cover the walls, echo the vines that often volunteer on the walls of Italian archaeological digs.

The Entry Path continues to wind its way along the side of the canyon, offering carefully planned glimpses or vignettes of the Villa that allow the visitor a gradual discovery. The Villa's ornate façades are framed in clusters of Mediterranean trees such as cypress, olive, oleander, and pine, heightening the anticipation of arrival.

Finally, the walk opens out dramatically to reveal the classically inspired Outdoor Theater, a hemicycle carved into the hillside. Constructed of alternating tiers of pre-cast concrete and stone—and seating 450—the Theater is located in front of the Villa's façade. With its spiral columns, the façade thus acts as a scenic backdrop for the stage.

There was no theater at the ancient Villa dei Papiri. But the one here—modeled after some of the smaller theaters of the ancient world, such as those at Pompeii and at Segesta in Sicily—provides a memorable juxtaposition of buildings and spaces, acting as a kind of anteroom to the Villa itself. The Theater hosts performances of ancient plays and other cultural events, as permitted by the mild Southern California climate. Theater Plaza, the performance area, acts as a hub for the entire complex, a meeting point, and a place where large groups gather for orientation and other activities.

Alongside the fifteen tiers of theater seats are corresponding step planters overflowing with plants such as aromatic lavender; lavender cotton, with its delicate, globose flower heads; pink-flowered Dalmatian cranesbill; and the evergreen mat-forming globe daisy. Clipped cylinders of the evergreen dwarf myrtle punctuate the plantings.

Near the Villa are a bookshop, a partly underground 250-seat auditorium, as well as a café and a terrace, where visitors can relax over food and drink. The buildings are designed in a contemporary style of architecture, but one that references the classical vocabulary of the Villa. They revolve around an expansive rectangular pool with a fountain, all enclosed by high walls on three sides. Water wells up from the center of the pool, propagating gentle ripples out toward the pool's edge. The near, open side of the pool has an "infinity" edge—that is, no edging per se—so that the water simply runs over into a channel below. The planting of the pool is deliberately exotic and makes no reference to the plants of the Roman period. Tropical water lilies—some with unusual purple-and-green mottled leaves—and elephant ears (*Alocasia*), with their large arrow-shaped leaves and contrasting midribs and veins, impart a hint of tropical rainforest to the pool. The fountain connected to it consists of a "weeping wall," in which water seeps down the fountain's enclosing travertine walls to the pool below. The dripping water heightens the color of the travertine, causing it to glisten in the sunlight.

Located on the hill is the original Getty residence, known as the Ranch House, which now houses the Villa's curatorial and other staff. It is situated amid monumental specimens of blue-needled Atlantic cedar (*Cedrus atlantica*), an evergreen that originates in the Atlas Mountains of Morocco on the southern coast of the Mediterranean. There are also specimens of two native tree species, the Sierra redwood and the coast redwood. In the background, the high hills are covered with the wild chaparral vegetation of Topanga State Park in the Santa Monica Mountains.

Alocasia veitchii
ELEPHANT EAR
To 5 ft. (Borneo)

This Southeast Asia native is the tallest plant in the
fountain. The leaves are quite large, up to thirty
inches in length, hence the name ELEPHANT EAR.
This plant thrives in bog gardens where its roots
are covered with water or in a garden setting in rich
humic soil. It requires regular water if not planted
near or in a pond and cannot survive winter without
mild night temperatures. *Alocasia veitchii* is closely
related to taro, one of the oldest cultivated plants,
which is harvested for its fleshy roots. Today many
cultivars are available with varying leaf colors and
variegations. Does best in dappled shade. Hardy to
about 50°.

Bellis perennis
ENGLISH DAISY
2–8 in. (Europe)

This DAISY is part of the meadow mixture that surrounds countless ancient Roman sites. At the Getty Villa it can be seen in front of the Museum along the Entry Path and on the rooftop of the parking structure, where it has naturalized. Romans knew of its astringent properties. They found it growing throughout Europe, and wherever they were in battle, they pressed the flowers and used the juice on wounds. Today it is prescribed in homeopathy for pain and soreness during pregnancy. Lower-body joint pain is also improved with a tincture of this herb. The ENGLISH DAISY wants full sun in areas with relatively cool summers and will grow in any type of soil. Hardy to about −20°.

Campanula glomerata
GLOBE BELLFLOWER
To 18 in. (Turkey, Europe)

This eastern Mediterranean native grows at the base of the Outdoor Theater along with the much taller CHIMNEY BELLFLOWER. The GLOBE BELLFLOWER blooms from May through August. The flowers are arranged in a spherical head, ranging in color from deep purple to pale lavender and white, on a short hairy stalk. The Romans used this plant to attract honeybees. Today it is planted in woodland gardens and has naturalized in meadows throughout Great Britain. It thrives in full sun but will tolerate partial sun and likes well-drained soil. Hardy to about −30°.

Campanula portenschlagiana (C. muralis)
DALMATIAN BELLFLOWER
To 4 in. (Balkan Peninsula)

Found throughout the eastern Mediterranean but native to the Dalmatian Mountains in Croatia, this species spreads from clumps. The visitor can find it planted along the Entry Path as an edging against the wall. Both flowers and leaves have been collected and eaten since ancient times. They have a very mild taste and are harvested fresh for use in salads. BELLFLOWER motifs appear in art from ancient Greek times on. The star-shaped flower is readily distinguished in wreaths, garlands, jewelry, and frescoes. It thrives in sun or light shade and needs well-drained soil. Hardy to about −20°.

Centranthus ruber
JUPITER'S BEARD
To 36 in. (Mediterranean)

This Mediterranean native can be found growing in poor, alkaline soil and in rocky crevices throughout the ancient Roman world. Pink flowers are most common, but white flowers occur naturally as well. It is very drought tolerant and can also be invasive, as it reseeds readily. Many ancient sites have JUPITER'S BEARD growing in cracks in limestone columns and lintels. At the Villa, it grows along the Entry Path, spilling down the hillside toward the Herb Garden. Although rather bitter, the entire plant is edible. The Romans used the roots and leaves in stews. Hardy to about −10°.

Convolvulus cneorum
BUSH MORNING GLORY
To 4 ft. (Central and western Mediterranean)

Another plant commonly found among ancient ruins, BUSH MORNING GLORY can be found growing in limestone cracks and alkaline soils. This describes many ancient sites from Italy and western Europe to the Iberian Peninsula, where this plant is native. The MORNING GLORY motif was incorporated into pavement patterns in North Africa during the Roman period. The small white hairs on the leaves help to protect the plant from drying out by collecting morning dew and shading the leaf surface from the sun. This plant requires very little water, which makes it highly adaptable to the Southern California climate. It likes full, hot sun and well-drained soil. Hardy to about 20°.

Coreopsis lanceolata
TICKSEED
To 24 in. (Central and southern United States)

In the spring, this perennial meadow plant turns the Great Plains into a sea of yellow. At the Villa, it grows on the rooftop garden above the parking structure and along the entry road in front of the Museum. It reseeds readily and is very drought tolerant, which makes it perfect for dry meadow gardens. TICKSEED is a food source for many insects, including several butterfly caterpillars, beetles, and moths. The monarch butterflies that rest at the Villa in the early spring months find this plant along their Pacific migration path. Plant in full sun in any soil. Hardy to about −30°.

Cupressus sempervirens
ITALIAN CYPRESS
To 70 ft. (Eastern Mediterranean, Iran)

Originally associated with mourning and the rulers of the Underworld, this tree was planted next to grave markers throughout the Roman empire. Boughs were placed before the home of the deceased as a warning: no sacred rite was to be performed in the presence of a dead body. The body was later placed on CYPRESS branches before interment. According to Theophrastus this tree was particularly abundant in Crete, Lycia, and Rhodes. Ovid described the tree and attributed the origin of its name to Cyparissus, a young boy and favorite of Apollo who so grieved for his pet deer that the god turned him into a CYPRESS. The tree is still revered in Christian traditions. Grows in sun or partial shade in any soil. Hardy to about 15°.

Echium candicans (E. fastuosum)
PRIDE OF MADEIRA
To 6 ft. (Madeira Islands)

This plant is native to the dry rocky slopes of the Madeira Islands in the Atlantic. It was planted by ancient Romans to attract bees. The resulting honey is highly prized for its flavor, even today. The plant is very drought tolerant, and its large clusters of blue flowers can be found blooming above the Entry Path and Outdoor Theater in the spring. It requires no summer water, so it is a good choice for water-sensitive gardens. PRIDE OF MADEIRA has a short life span (usually less than 10 years) but reseeds readily and produces successive generations each year as it ages. Plant in dry, gravelly soil and full sun. May need summer water in warmer areas. Hardy to about 20°.

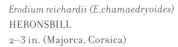

Erodium reichardii (E.chamaedryoides)
HERONSBILL
2–3 in. (Majorca, Corsica)

The scientific name for this plant is derived from the ancient Greek word for heron, because its seed-pod resembles the bird's sharp beak. This alpine plant plays an important role in the life cycle of moths. Its small flowers and tight, concise foliage can be seen edging the Entry Path and in the Herb Garden. HERONSBILL survives with no summer water in its natural habitat but looks best with regular irrigation. Plant in full sun or partial shade in dry, well-drained soil. Hardy to about 10°.

Euphorbia characias wulfenii
SPURGE
To 4 ft. (Southeastern Europe)

Although this subspecies is from southeastern
Europe, other euphorbias are native to many other
Mediterranean areas. SPURGE thrives on seasonal
water only and has no pests, due to its toxic milky
sap. It was named by King Juba II of Mauretania
for the ancient Greek physician Euphorbus, who
found the plant growing in the Atlas Mountains.
Dioscorides also described this plant and attributed several medicinal uses to it. SPURGE provides food for many butterfly and moth species.
SPURGE likes full sun and dry, gravelly soil. Hardy
to about 10°.

Globularia meridionalis
GLOBE DAISY
4–8 in. (Southeastern Alps, Apennine Mountains, Balkan Peninsula)

This plant can be seen growing at the base of the Outdoor Theater wall. It blooms all year and can spread as wide as 4 ft. It forms a low mat of foliage and is very cold tolerant, as it is native to the high mountains of southern Europe. It is a favorite of honeybees and is planted with BELLFLOWERS, whose nectar can be collected in the same season. Dioscorides wrote about this plant and its medicinal properties, but these uses have not been verified. Must have full sun and tolerates a wide range of soils. Hardy to about −10°.

Lathyrus latifolius
PERENNIAL PEA
To 6 ft. (Europe, northwestern Africa, Caucasus)

This perennial grows in the olive terraces, where it has thrived since the Villa opened in 1974. The soft pink flowers cascade down the stone wall throughout the spring and summer months. The ancient Romans used it for livestock fodder. They also knew that when it was planted with other crops, the crop yield improved. This is because, like many legumes, it fixes nitrogen, making the nutrient available in the soil. Unlike other PEA family members, it has no fragrance. It is a food source for many butterflies and moths. Needs full sun and may be planted in a wide range of soils. Hardy to about −20°.

Parthenocissus tricuspidata
BOSTON IVY
Vine (Eastern Asia, Japan, Korea)

This vine grows on the wall along the Entry Path. Native to Asia, it has been planted in North America since colonial times. It is used to cover stone and brick buildings in temperate areas such as Boston, Massachusetts, hence its common name. IVY attaches itself to masonry walls with little pads on its stem tendrils. This tenacious mechanism, once established, can support vines up to 6 in. thick. Annual thinning keeps the oldest, heaviest vines from damaging the masonry. Fall is the best season for this plant, due to its brilliant scarlet foliage. Thrives in full sun to full shade in any kind of soil. Hardy to about −20°.

Pinus canariensis
CANARY ISLAND PINE
To 80 ft. (Canary Islands)

This tall, slender pine thrives in sandy soil in coastal areas and is the most drought tolerant of all pines. Being a subtropical native, it does not like cold temperatures and will quickly die of frost when planted out of its temperate range. In Greek mythology, PINES were the favorite tree of Rhea, mother of Zeus. Dioscorides suggested that pine sap be added to wine. This practice is still common today in the production of Greek retsina wines. Plant in full sun in well-drained soil. Hardy to about 30°.

Quercus suber
CORK OAK
To 70 ft. (Western Mediterranean, North Africa)

This distinctive tree can be seen along the Entry Path at the south end near the stairs. The thick spongy bark has been used for centuries to make corks for bottles. The trees must be around 25–35 years old to produce the first crop of viable cork. Today these trees are grown in groves throughout Spain, Portugal, and North Africa. They require carefully trained workers to harvest the outer bark while preserving the inner, vital layers of the tree. To the Romans, the OAK leaf symbolized the highest honor that could be bestowed. Emperors and deities were depicted wearing wreaths of OAK leaves on their heads. Needs full sun and dry, well-drained soil. Hardy to about 20°.

Rosa 'Ballerina'
BALLERINA MUSK ROSE
8–10 ft. (Garden origin)

This upright shrub ROSE, introduced in 1937 from
garden origin, is reminiscent of the MUSK ROSE
of antiquity. Its arching canes produce clusters of
pink flowers with white centers. Less fragrant than
other varieties, it has a very long blooming period,
from spring through the end of fall. The orange
rose hips that develop under each spent flower are
rich in vitamin C and have been used as a cold rem
edy and as an expectorant. This recent introduction
is just one example of the diversity and popularity
ROSES have enjoyed throughout recorded history.
It requires full sun and rich, humic, well-drained
soil. Hardy to about −10°.

Rosa 'Scepter'd Isle'
SCEPTER'D ISLE ROSE
8–10 ft. canes (Garden origin)

This modern ROSE introduction, from the David
Austin Series, dates from 1996. It blooms throughout the summer months. As the flower ages, it
opens to reveal its yellow stamens. SCEPTER'D
ISLE ROSES contribute to the fragrant pathway that
leads to the Outdoor Theater. Many aromatic plants
grow along this promenade entice visitors' senses
as they approach the Museum Entrance. These
ROSES are not pruned down as severely in the winter as many other varieties, and their flowers will
persist into the cold months. Give it full sun, rich,
well-drained soil, and plenty of nutrients. Hardy to
about −10°.

Santolina rosmarinifolia (S. virens)
GREEN LAVENDER COTTON
To 24 in. (Southwestern Europe)

This Mediterranean native is particularly drought tolerant. Its bright yellow flowers were used by the Romans as a textile dye. Because of its aromatic foliage, GREEN LAVENDER COTTON has been used since antiquity to repel fleas and moths and was planted at doorways for this purpose. It has been planted in knot gardens since medieval times due to its tight growth habit and quick response to pruning and can be shaped into desired forms with relatively little care. The plant grows well in full sun or partial shade and requires very little water to look its best. Hardy to about −10°.

Vinca major
PERIWINKLE
18 in. (Western Mediterranean)

This plant is native to coastal areas from Spain, France, and North Africa to the western Caucasus. It is employed as a ground cover between the Entry Path and the Herb Garden, where it holds the steep hillside in place. PERIWINKLE has been used for centuries in the treatment of blood sugar problems. It has astringent and sedative properties and also affects high blood pressure. The Romans wove garlands with vines and flowers such as these to festoon their peristyle courtyards for parties and celebrations. Will tolerate full sun to full shade and any type of soil, although it can be invasive. Hardy to about 0°.

Nymphaea sp.
WATER LILIES
(tropical species and hybrids)

The WATER LILIES and other bog plants in this
area are from New World tropical settings. The
favorite LILY hybrids are the red-leaved 'Director
George T. Moore' and 'Foxfire' and the white 'Alba.'
Other bog plants that merit attention include the
pink-hued variegated leaves of *Oenanthe javanica*
'Flamingo' planted in the shallow trough at the
sides and the bronze-veined leaves of *Alocasia*,
or ELEPHANT EAR. Being tropical, these plants
like full sun and look their best in the warm summer months. Many of these lilies do not survive
the temperate winters in Southern California and
are replaced each spring. The leaves of the hardier
varieties, however, withstand the low temperatures
and continue to float on the water surface, provid-
ing protection from the cold for the fish during the
winter months. Divide and fertilize in the spring
before the growing season. Plant in sand for best
results. Hardiness varies.

THE INNER PERISTYLE GARDEN

From the Museum Entrance, an axial view opens up through the Villa's Atrium. The visitor's eye is led to the first garden courtyard, called the Inner Peristyle Garden, then through an indoor lobby area, and finally to a distant view of the fountains of the Villa's East Garden. The courtyard is thus the first of the Villa's individual gardens that the visitor sees.

The Inner Peristyle Garden, a cool, semi-enclosed space surrounded by richly decorated two-story architecture, is modeled after the gardens of the Villa dei Papiri. The focus of this garden is a long, narrow central pool, lined with white marble. Two low, matching jets of water create surface ripples along the length of the pool.

Life-size bronze figures of maidens—replicas of those excavated in the Villa dei Papiri—stand in semicircular indents along the pool's length. The original figures were found in the Outer Peristyle of the Villa dei Papiri; the decision to place the replicas in the Getty Villa's Inner Peristyle Garden is therefore aesthetic rather than archaeological. Each sculpture represents a young woman dressed in a *peplos*, an outer garment worn by women in ancient Greece. For this reason, the figures are called *peplophoroi*, or *"peplos* wearers." Each individual figure casts its own reflection in the pool, and the dark bronze color stands out against the pale tones of the surrounding building.

The hard edges of the marble pool are softened with a band of planting that consists of clumps of Siberian iris alternating with English ivies trained over wire frames of galvanized steel to form low mounds. Although called English ivy, this plant is native all over Europe and is certainly appropriate for a Roman-style garden. The ivies are grown in clay pots that are sunk into the ground so that their aggressive roots do not spread into, and impoverish, the adjoining plantings. It takes about eighteen months for the ivy to grow over and cover the wire frames. The sword-like leaves and the purple spring flowers of the Siberian iris contrast effectively with the rounded ivy mounds and create a delicate visual rhythm around the pool.

The overall garden plan follows a traditional formula. A central axial pool and a corresponding cross-axial walkway divide the garden into four quarters. Each quarter is made up of one large planting bed. The focus of each bed is a bay laurel tree that is pruned carefully three times a year so that its evergreen foliage retains an even, globose shape atop a tall, clear stem. The bay laurels, all matching in shape and size, are grown in raised concrete planters that are painted Pompeian red. Because the garden lies on top of the Villa's lower level, it has only a shallow layer of soil. Therefore, the circular planters are raised in order to give the laurels a sufficiently deep root run. A carpet of gray-green chamomile clothes the soil inside the planters, while a darker green hedge of the large-leaved butcher's broom screens their sides.

Apart from the laurels, no plant in this garden is allowed to grow more than three feet tall. Each bed is framed by a perimeter hedge of aromatic rosemary, whose fine, gray foliage acts as a foil for the dark green leaves of the plants in the bed's interior. The latter consists mainly of dwarf myrtle and Italian buckthorn, clipped into cylinders and balls that are arranged informally but in melded combinations. This small-scale mat foliage contrasts effectively with the loose, more-fluid growth and larger, shinier leaves of neighboring hellebores and acanthus. The quiet green flowers of the hellebores brighten the garden in winter, while the acanthus sends up its purple-and-white flower spikes in summer. (The acanthus leaf inspired many decorative motifs in antiquity and, more recently, at the Getty Villa—see, for example, the acanthus motif in the ceiling of the room known as the Basilica.) Near ground level, grassy bulb foliage sets off the low, rounded leaves of violets. Mat-forming creeping jenny creates a contrast with the taller plants.

The garden derives much of its visual interest from foliage textures and forms rather than from flower color. However, the harmony of quiet foliage greens is complemented through the seasons with flowers in white and pastel colors only. White snowflakes follow the pale blue flowers of the early-spring grape hyacinths. The snowflakes are followed, in summer, by white-flowered Madonna lilies, one of the oldest cultivated plants. (There are depictions of Madonna lilies in murals dating from ca. 1500 B.C. in the Minoan palace at Knossos on Crete.) What appear to be casually placed groups of bellflowers, so called on account of the shape of their flowers, add color accents to the beds throughout the summer. They are seen in three different species, two in creeping form—one blue-flowered, the other white-flowered—and the third also blue-flowered but of an upright form. Also elegant in summer is the purple-flowered foxglove, so called because each tubular flower fits over a finger like a glove. Clumps of lavender-blue scabious, sometimes called pincushion flower for its protruding stamens, also add their color. Most of the violas that flower in mats at ground level are of the usual violet-colored kind, but some white forms are also seen. In autumn, the jewel-like red berries of the small-leaved butcher's broom and the black berries of the myrtles reveal themselves beneath their evergreen foliage. As in the other gardens of the Villa, redwood headers are set in the soil of each bed to separate the different planting areas—one for annuals and perennials, and another for bulbs.

In addition to its planting, each quarter of the garden is ornamented with decorative sculptural elements. A pair of life-size bronze portrait busts, part of the collection representing ancient Greek military and civic leaders, athletes, philosophers, poets, and literary figures—copies of originals from the Villa dei Papiri—are placed in each quarter. They are mounted on white Carrara-marble posts that raise them to eye level, as was the practice in antiquity. (Carrara marble, quarried in Tuscany, is noted for its pure white color.) A final ornament in each quarter is a birdbath, also carved in white Carrara marble and supplied by Ditta Medici, a venerable marble workshop in Rome. Raised on pedestals, also of marble, the birdbaths were designed after a description by Karl Weber. The originals, found during his excavations of the Villa dei Papiri, were later lost, but not before they were illustrated in a book entitled *Observations sur les antiquites de la ville d'Herculaneum* (1754) by Charles-Nicolas Cochin and Jérôme-Charles Bellicard. Cochin was a French artist who accompanied Abel-François Poisson— the brother of Madame de Pompadour, mistress of King Louis XV of France—on a visit to Italy, where he made a study of the antiquities. From the center of each birdbath, a low jet of water bubbles up and splashes gently into the basin, which overflows into a shallow square pool at ground level. The pool is framed within alternating bands of marble chips and mat-forming herbs such as thyme and penny royal, with vertical strips of white marble in between.

Each of these elements in this shady garden—the strong architectural background, the sparkle of the fountains, the dark bronze statuary, and the white birdbaths— enlivens the calm symmetry of design and planting and the understated evergreen hues of the trees and shrubs. Seasonal flower colors in each of the garden's four planting beds add highlights throughout the year.

Campanula poscharskyana
SERBIAN BELLFLOWER
2–6 in. (Balkan Peninsula)

This plant is native to the Carpathian Mountains of present-day Serbia. It thrives in full sun as well as partial shade, which makes it a perfect choice to maintain the balance and symmetry of the Inner Peristyle Garden, with its varying light conditions. This perennial blooms all year and was incorporated into ancient Greek wreaths. The stems and leaves are edible, though slightly bitter, and were used as salad greens in ancient Rome. Does well in any soil. Hardy to about −30°.

Campanula pyramidalis
CHIMNEY BELLFLOWER
To 8 ft. (Italy, northwestern Balkan Peninsula)

The botanical name, like the common name, de-scribes the bell shape of this flower, which towers above all other in the garden and can have up to 100 blossoms per stalk, making it a favorite plant for honeybees. It blooms in blue and white all year but primarily in spring and summer. Native to rocky, exposed limestone environments in the southeast-ern Mediterranean, it thrives in the sandy soil on the sunny side of the Inner Peristyle Garden. In this setting, staking is required to hold the plant up. Plant in full sun. It wants well-drained, grav-elly, alkaline soil. Hardy to about 0°.

Digitalis purpurea
FOXGLOVE
To 4 ft. (Europe, western and central Asia, northwestern Africa)

This plant can be found in partial shade at meadow's edge throughout Europe. It likes to be sheltered from the noonday sun. The spotted flowers, arrayed in spikes, range from purple to pink to white. Blooming from March through July, FOXGLOVE is a food source for many moths and butterflies. It is named for the finger-like shape of the flowers. Although known to be toxic, it has been used in small quantities since medieval times for reviving a weak heart rate and in modern homeopathic medicine for heart-related ailments. Plant in rich loam, in partially shaded, woodland environs. Hardy to about −20°.

Hedera helix
ENGLISH IVY
Vine (Europe)

The IVY domes surrounding the central fountain are formed using a wire frame. In antiquity, creating unusual forms and manipulating nature— fashioning IVY topiaries, for example—was a way of demonstrating man's dominion over the natural world. In Greek mythology, the god Dionysos was saved from Hera's wrath by his nurse, who screened his crib with IVY. Romans associated the plant with Bacchus and included vines of GRAPE and IVY in most artwork depicting him. In modern times IVY has been associated with quality spirits and breweries. Grows well in full sun to full shade, in any soil. Hardy to about 0°.

Lysimachia nummularia
CREEPING JENNY
2 in. (Southern Europe)

This plant, native to sylvan settings throughout southern Europe, thrives in the shady corners of the Inner Peristyle Garden. The splash of the fountain keeps the stems and leaves constantly misted, which they welcome. CREEPING JENNY can also be found in the High Sierra, where it was introduced by Europeans. It was named by Dioscorides to commemorate Lysimachus (ca. 355–281 B.C.), a companion and successor to Alexander the Great who used the plant to treat battle wounds of his soldiers. Dioscorides prescribed it for bleeding and dysentery, and Pliny the Elder also wrote about it. Plant in full shade, in rich moist soil. Hardy to about −30°.

Ruscus hypoglossum
RUSCUS
To 18 in. (Italy, Czech Republic, Turkey)

This plant and its relatives were named in ancient Greek times by Theophrastus. He described RUSCUS as peculiar because its bright red fruit is borne on the leaves, which are actually modified stems, or cladophylls. The tiny inconspicuous flowers first develop in the same unusual position, where the fruit then develops, mostly in female plants. The tender new growth was collected and used fresh in salads, a practice still common today in northern Europe. RUSCUS can also be sculpted into a hedge, making it a prized plant for the shade garden. The plant is very drought tolerant. It does best in full shade and grows in any soil. Hardy to about 10°.

Scabiosa columbaria 'Butterfly Blue'
SMALL SCABIOUS (PINCUSHION FLOWER)
20–28 in. (Europe, western Asia)

In ancient Rome, honey was a valuable commodity as the primary sweetener. It was common to cultivate flowering plants whose nectar attracted bees. PINCUSHION FLOWER is attractive to butterflies, moths, and honeybees alike. It is native to all of Europe and can be seen blooming in meadow settings, including many ancient temple sites throughout Greece. The plant has a long blooming season, lasting from spring through the summer months, and blooms best on the sunny side of the garden, since it likes full sun. Plant in rich, well-drained soil. Hardy to about −30°.

Soleirolia soleirolii
BABY'S TEARS
2 in. (Western Mediterranean)

This plant was first discovered in Corsica by the French botanist Joseph-François Soleirol, for whom it is named. It is also found throughout Italy growing in rocky crevices where moisture collects. It thrives in shady environs such as the spring area near the front gate of the Villa and by the corner fountains in the Inner Peristyle Garden. BABY'S TEARS lends itself to pruning and shaping. Romans were keen on displaying their pruning talent and may have used plants like this for such a purpose. Due to its tender herbaceous nature, there would be no enduring evidence of its use. Plant in full shade in moist, humic soil. Hardy to about 0°.

THE EAST GARDEN

In the report of his excavations, Karl Weber noted what appeared to be a small garden adjoining the Villa dei Papiri. A modest, secluded garden for the enjoyment of a villa's owner, his family, and his intimate friends is thought to have been a typical feature of Roman villas. It is this kind of private sanctuary that the East Garden of the Getty Villa is designed to evoke.

A pair of solid bronze doors, with a columned porch (the East Porch) inspired by an example at the Villa San Marco at Stabiae overlooking the Bay of Naples, marks the entry to the garden, which is enclosed within high walls that ensure a sense of privacy and tranquillity. Its white-painted walls stand out sharply against the dark green of the canyon vegetation behind. The upright projections (merlons) that occur at intervals along the top of the walls are typical of ancient Roman boundary and garden walls. Bronze latticework gates, framed by Corinthian pilasters, open onto the woodland at either end of the garden.

The focal point at the center of the garden is a cast-concrete bowl, raised high on a pedestal and brimming with water. Set into the sides of the bowl are eight bronze feline heads, copies of originals that were found in the atrium of the Villa dei Papiri. From the mouths of these heads, whose patina is now a fine verdigris, water falls into a circular, marble-edged basin below. Clumps of water-loving plants provide accents. Vertical sheaves of leaves of water irises contrast with the flat leaf-pads of water lilies. The lily pads also act as foils for groups of a water-loving plant called "arrowhead" due to the shape of its leaves. The blue and purple flowers of the water lilies—grown in underwater pots so they do not become invasive—and the purple and red flowers of the water irises provide rich color accents in season. An encircling band of evergreen butcher's broom, so called because butchers once used its branches to sweep the sawdust from their floors, softens the pool base.

Circling the fountain is aggregate-seeded walkway. At the margins of this walkway are four cast-concrete benches, whose curves reflect the circular shape of the pool. Painted Pompeian red, they are inset into plant beds along the walkway.

A secondary focal point is provided by an exuberant mosaic- and shell-lined fountain set in one of the garden's external walls. It is a painstakingly reconstructed replica of a fixture from the House of the Great Fountain in Pompeii. The facing is made of intricate mosaics composed of tesserae of marble, lava stone, and glass in various colors, with blue predominating. Seashells define the outlines of the various mosaic patterns—scrolls, swags, and lozenges. They also set off images of plants and birds as well as of urns and other decorative motifs. A mosaic in the fountain's central niche depicts a wild-haired god surrounded by reeds, thought to represent Okeanos (or the Ocean). Below it, water cascades down a narrow flight of white marble steps into a pool below. On either side of the central niche, larger than life-size theater masks, carved in white marble and hollowed-out behind, are positioned prominently. One represents Hercules with his lion skin; the head of the lion partly covers the back of Hercules' head. The other represents a tragic figure portrayed with characteristic unkempt hair. Both the mosaics and the marble sculptures were fabricated in the town of Pietrasanta in Tuscany, the former by Favret Artistic Mosaics, the latter by the Palla Studio. The whole ensemble strikes a note of whimsy or fantasy in a sequence of gardens at the Getty Villa that is otherwise notable for its restraint.

As with the Inner Peristyle Garden, the East Garden is divided into quarters by axial and cross-axial walkways. Each quarter comprises two planting beds divided by a pathway. The smaller of the two beds is roughly triangular and is adjacent to the central fountain; the larger, rectangular, bed is located toward the garden's perimeter.

The keynote planting in each quarter consists of a group of London plane trees of the disease-resistant 'Columbia' variety. The London plane tree (*Platanus acerifolia*) is closely related to the oriental plane (*Platanus orientalis*) that is shown in a garden scene painted on the walls of Empress Livia's house at Prima Porta, outside Rome. This tree was much prized in the ancient Roman garden for its abundant shade. The London plane is also closely related to the California sycamore. In general, plane trees are an excellent choice for a restricted space like the East Garden, since they can be pruned frequently and effectively without loss of vigor.

These plane trees are grouped in the East Garden with bay laurels, which are also associated with the ancient Roman garden. As in the Inner Peristyle Garden, the foliage of the bay laurels is clipped into a globe form above a clear stem. The repeated use of such similar plantings throughout the Villa gardens underlines the continuity of style from one individual garden to another.

The garden's beds are edged with dwarf hedges of butcher's broom. A botanical peculiarity, worth noticing in season, is that its flowers and berries emerge not from the stem but from the center of the leaf. The interiors of the beds are accented with clipped obelisks of English holly and mounds of English ivy, which, like the shaped bay laurels, echo similar plantings in the Inner Peristyle Garden. The dense growth of the laurel and ivy acts as a foil for the loose clusters of bear's breech and hellebore. The hellebore species used in this garden is the Corsican hellebore, also called the Corsican rose. Spreading along the ground between the taller plants are mats of low-growing feverfew, thyme, and viola. Clumps of crocus and snowflake in spring, iris and foxglove (both purple and white) in summer, and cyclamen in autumn add their seasonal color. The most striking flowering plant in these beds is the Peruvian squill, a spring-flowering Mediterranean native (despite its name, it does not come from Peru). Its pyramidal blue racemes give the beds a strangely exotic aspect when the plant is in flower.

Against the long white walls of the garden's perimeter extend long, narrow beds. One of them contains a rhythmical line of evergreen Italian buckthorn, clipped into a buttress shape. Along the wall of the Villa, there is a similarly rhythmical line of large terracotta pots. Of traditional Italian style, with a heavy lip to make transportation easy, these pots are filled with matching specimens of the dwarf strawberry tree. Against the adjoining walls are beds edged with boxwood, containing the pale green, semitranslucent fronds of bird's nest ferns, named for the tight, nest-like clumps formed by their large simple leaves.

With the dappled shadows of the plane trees playing in ever-changing complex patterns on the garden's white perimeter walls and the sound of water splashing in its fountains, the East Garden is a place for peaceful contemplation, just as the similarly located garden of the Villa dei Papiri must have been some two thousand years ago.

Cyclamen hederifolium
BABY CYCLAMEN
4–6 in. (Eastern Mediterranean, Asia Minor)

This cool-season bloomer grows in abundance in Europe and Turkey. Locally it is called the ALPINE VIOLET, because it is found in shady areas in the mountains, usually in a layer of mulch. It grows from a large tuber just under the soil surface and blooms when the days are shortening. The flowers bloom facing down, and the petals are recurved upward from a pentagonal throat. As the flower is spent, the stem coils down to the ground like a spring. The leaves are mottled green and silver, possibly to camouflage the plant and deter grazing animals. Plant in full to partial shade in rich, humic soil. Hardy to about −10°.

Helleborus argutifolius
CORSICAN HELLEBORE
24–36 in. (Corsica, Sardinia)

This plant has an interesting growth pattern in that
each year's growth is produced on a new stalk aris-
ing from the crown. The chartreuse flowers linger
for several months as a new year's flush of foliage
emerges. This plant needs shade to perform well.
At the Villa, the shade provided by the SYCAMORES
helps the HELLEBORES when the summer sun is
intense. The plant is toxic but Pliny the Elder
reports that it was used as a cure for madness as
well as a poison. Modern varieties involving other
species have blossoms that range in color from
white to pink and purple. It needs neutral to alkaline soil. Hardy to about −10°.

Ilex aquifolium
ENGLISH HOLLY
To 80 ft. (Western and southern Europe,
North Africa, western Asia)

This Christmas favorite is found in mixed wood-lands throughout temperate Europe. Its genus name has been used since antiquity, but in reference to the holly oak (*Quercus ilex*) rather than this plant. It is dioecious, meaning that each plant has either male or female flowers, not both. Males and females must be planted close together for the flowers to pollinate each other and produce berries and seeds. The red berries are a food source for many birds. The wood has long been used for carving and woodworking. The plant can be used as a diuretic but is generally considered toxic. There are several variegated forms with cream-colored margins. Likes full sun to partial shade and rich, well-drained soil. Hardy to about 20°.

Iris ensata 'Variegata'
JAPANESE WATER IRIS 'VARIEGATA'
To 4 ft. (North China, Japan, eastern Russia)

Named for the many colored flowers, this aquatic
variety is available in yellow, blue, white, or purple. The foliage can be striped with white or simply
green. The white stripes on the foliage are caused
by a plant virus that halts the production of green
chlorophyll along certain areas, which produces
the stripes. The blooming period is early spring,
but the visitor may find purple flowers occasion-
ally throughout the summer months. These plants
require regular water if planted in a garden setting.
A bog or pond environment is preferred. Hardy
to −10°.

Iris x Louisiana 'Ann Chowning'
LOUISIANA
To 4 ft. (Garden origin)

In Greek mythology, Iris was the messenger of the
gods and also the rainbow goddess. This genus is
extremely varied and includes plants native to all
continents except Antarctica. The LOUISIANA IRIS
is adapted to life with its roots submerged in water.
Today the plant is enjoyed in the East Garden where
it attracts dragonflies and other aquatic insects. In
recent years many new cultivars have been introduced, offering gardeners interesting new flower
colors. In a water garden, these plants perform
best in full sun. Given the proper environment they
require little care and have very few pests. Hardy to
about −20°.

Iris pseudacorus
YELLOW FLAG
To 4 ft. (Europe, Asia, Asia Minor)

This plant, native to Britain, western Europe, and east to Siberia, lives in shallow water or wet meadows. This IRIS has water-dispersed seeds but can tolerate prolonged dry periods. It grows well with other bog plants and blooms for most of the year. It has been used in water-treatment processes because the roots have the ability to take up heavy metals. There are usually areas of brown or purple pigment on each flower. YELLOW FLAG is a very vigorous grower and can be invasive if left unchecked. To maximize blooms, plant in full sun. Needs rich soil. Hardy to about −20°.

Platanus x acerifolia 'Columbia'
LONDON PLANE
To 70 ft. (Garden origin)

In the East Garden, these trees are pruned with a sculpting technique called pollarding, in which each year's growth is removed to the same point or hub. These hubs grow callus tissue that distorts the branch ends into knobs, which sprout new growth annually. The Romans were the first to practice this pruning technique. This modern variety was chosen for its resistance to several common problems, such as powdery mildew and anthracnose, a fungal disease that affects the leaves. Removing all leaves and stems at the end of each growing season is an excellent way of starting fresh each spring. Needs full sun and well-drained soil. Hardy to about −10°.
Rhamnus alaternus

ITALIAN BUCKTHORN
To 15 ft. (Portugal, Morocco, Mediterranean, Ukraine)

The BUCKTHORN gets its name from the spines on its stems. The entire genus has veins that curve upward toward the leaf tips. The bark has been used for centuries to make dye, though there is no evidence it was used as such in ancient times. It is the exclusive food source for the moth *Bucculatrix alaternella*. ITALIAN BUCKTHORN can be pruned into hedges or topiary forms and kept at a very short height if necessary. It can tolerate heat, wind, drought, or infrequent water, making it a valuable landscape shrub for many situations. Tolerates full sun to partial shade. Plant in humic soil with good drainage. Hardy to about 10°.

Ruscus aculeatus
BUTCHER'S BROOM
To 30 in. (Europe, northern Turkey to
North Africa, the Azores)

This plant has modified stems called cladophylls
that resemble leaves. The growing tips are collected to eat fresh in salads. It produces a small
white flower and then a red fruit in the center of
the cladophyll in female plants. It responds well to
pruning, so it makes an excellent hedge plant for
a shade garden. BUTCHER'S BROOM is a durable
plant that creates a dense root mass over time. It
can be divided easily once it is dislodged from its
growing site. It grows best in shade or partial shade
but can handle the midday window of direct sun in
the East Garden. It can survive on very little summer water and tolerates a wide range of soil conditions. Hardy to about 10°.

Scilla peruviana
PERUVIAN SQUILL
To 24 in. (Iberian Peninsula, Italy, North Africa)

Despite its name, this plant is native to the Mediterranean region. The first specimen was delivered
to Carolus Linnaeus (Carl von Linné), father of
modern taxonomy, for classification on the ship
Peru. Linnaeus confused the ship's name with the
region of origin, hence the erroneous plant name.
The foliage is visible for the entire year, while the
vibrant clusters of up to 100 blue flowers appear
in early spring and persist through April or May.
These bulbs have been planted under the ITALIAN
STONE PINES on either side of the Museum since
its founding and have never been disturbed. Plant
in partial sun to full shade in rich, humic soil with
good drainage. Hardy to about 20°.

Tanacetum parthenium
(or *Chrysanthemum parthenium*)
FEVERFEW
To 18 in. (Europe, the Caucasus)

This plant blooms for much of the year and can be found in most gardens at the Villa. It has aromatic foliage and daisy-like flowers and many medicinal uses. A decoction with sugar or honey is said to be good for coughs. A tincture made from FEVERFEW applied to insect bites relieves swelling and pain. An infusion of the flowers made with boiling water, allowed to cool, will allay pain associated with rheumatism. An infusion is also used to relieve earache. A soothing tonic of FEVERFEW calms the nerves. Thrives in full sun and does best in dry, gravelly soil. Hardy to about −10°.

Viola odorata
SWEET VIOLET
To 12 in. (Europe, North Africa, Asia up to
altitudes of 3,000 ft.)

These flowers are fragrant and have been used since
antiquity to flavor syrups and drinks. The plant has
been a constituent of perfumes since Roman times
and reached a zenith of popularity in the early
twentieth century. Leaves and flowers are used in
the treatment of respiratory ailments, principally
bronchitis. The edible VIOLET flowers are candied
as a confection and are used to decorate cakes and
salads. As a garden plant, it clumps and grows from
a central crown. It does not spread invasively by
runners, which makes it a good ground cover for
the shade garden. Likes partial sun to full shade
and the moist, calcareous soils of shady woodlands.
Hardy to about 0°.

THE OUTER PERISTYLE GARDEN

To enter the Outer Peristyle Garden, visitors pass through the sumptuously decorated room that the designers of the Museum based on the dining room of the Villa dei Papiri. A pair of massive bronze doors leads to steps that descend to garden level.

The extensive Outer Peristyle Garden is the principal garden of the Getty Villa. Its design is based closely on the outer peristyle garden of the Villa dei Papiri. Like that garden, the one at the Getty Villa is surrounded on all sides by a roofed colonnade, which acts as a visual frame for the garden as a whole. The repetitive rhythms of the Doric columns accentuate the great length of the colonnade (348 ft., or 106 m). The colonnade walls, decorated with illusionistic paintings in imitation of ancient Roman models, provide a brightly colored background to the garden.

The focus of the garden is a huge, rectangular central pool. It is approximately the size of the pool at the Villa dei Papiri, occupying nearly a third of the garden. In a Roman garden, such a pool would have been used for swimming or for breeding fish for the table. This pool, 210 feet (64 m) long with semicircular ends, offers a long unbroken vista down the center of the garden, further enhanced by the fact that the pool has been kept free of planting and that the three fountain jets and two recumbent bronze sculptures are low and unobtrusive.

The pool is raised two feet above ground level for the practical reason that it overlies a parking garage. However, this has the happy result of bringing the reflections of the surroundings closer to eye level. In particular, the pool acts as a mirror to the sky, bringing its light and color down into the center of the garden. The effect is augmented by the pale blue paint applied to the pool interior. The low bubbling of the three fountain jets—spaced evenly along the length of the pool—and the breezes blowing off the Pacific Ocean cause the surface of the water to ripple gently.

Like the other statuary in the garden, the bronze sculptures in the pool are cast from molds of original bronzes excavated at the Villa dei Papiri. At the near end of the pool, the figure of a beardless young satyr is shown sleeping on a rock of rough-cut travertine. At the far end, the figure of an older drunken satyr, head thrown back, finger pointing to the sky, reclines on a similar block of stone. The rough cut of the travertine gives an air of naturalism to the figures and provides a dramatic visual contrast to the smooth plane of water and the polished marble of the pool's surround.

The low wall retaining the pool is softened visually with a band of planting around its perimeter. Hedged with clipped boxwood, the perimeter band is planted with clusters of white Florentine iris alternating with mounds of English ivy, all growing above a carpet of creeping chamomile. As in the Inner Peristyle Garden, the vertical sword-like leaves of the irises pair dynamically with the low mounds of English ivy, establishing a stylistic continuity between the two gardens.

Surrounding this planting band are the main walkways of the garden. These are surfaced with exposed aggregate concrete using quarter-inch crushed gravel. Along the outer edge of the walkways, boxwood hedges, corresponding to those along the inner edge, extend along the length of the garden. The outer hedges enclose the garden's main planting beds, in which substantial trees and shrubs alternate with decorative garden structures, giving a strong vertical dimension to the garden's otherwise low planting. Cross paths, also edged with boxwood, lead to openings in the garden's perimeter walls, so that visitors catch glimpses of the canyon vegetation beyond.

A pair of venerable, multi-stemmed pomegranate trees, symmetrically planted on either side of the central axis, dominates the section of the garden nearest the Villa. With their scarlet flowers and subsequent large red fruit, these trees catch the eye in season. Year-round interest is provided by their gnarled and mottled trunks and by the traditional goblet shape into which they are sculpted. The latter allows light and air into the interior of the trees so the fruit ripens evenly. Now that their shape is fully formed, the trees require only an annual tip-pruning to maintain it.

The pomegranates are grown in raised circular concrete planters (painted Pompeian red) so that the trees have a sufficiently deep root run over the ancillary building structure that underlies the garden. Nearby, also grown in planters, are matching groups of oleanders of the natural species with single pink flowers. The sides of these planters are partially screened by discreet box hedges.

Completing the entry area's rich plantings are combinations of clipped myrtle and rosemary, with ivy mounds and acanthus clumps playing supporting roles. Mats of violet, thyme, and chamomile cover the ground between the taller plants.

The ornaments in the garden's entry area include a pair of lifelike bronze deer, placed symmetrically among the oleanders. Cast by the Chiurazzi foundry, like the other bronzes, they are elegantly proportioned, their heads raised as if suddenly alert. Nearby, a pair of diagonally aligned walkways lead to recessed, almost circular, seats with enlarged lion-paw ends made in cast stone. Their design, derived from seats excavated in a public area of Pompeii, was crafted into a mold by the late Henry Greutert, a local sculptor. The seats encircle pavement laid in an intricate geometrical pattern of contrasting triangular pieces of black slate and white limestone. Known as a "spinning wheel" pattern, it radiates from the center in ever-increasing circles.

The first of the substantial decorative features of the garden appears along the poolside paths: a pair of matching arbors, square in plan, one on either side of the central pool and opposite the first of the pool's fountain jets. Based on ancient Roman models, the arbors are constructed of four cast-concrete posts, painted white above and Pompeian red below, supporting crossbars of

rough-sawn redwood. Grapevines, trained in spirals around the posts, leaf out and later fruit luxu-
riantly in season. In the shade of each arbor is a cast-concrete bench, also painted Pompeian red.
On either side of the arbors are life-size bronze busts on white marble shafts, part of the collection
of such busts copied from originals found in the Villa dei Papiri.

Farther along the paths, and opposite the middle fountain jet, are matching pairs of mature
date palms, one pair on either side of the pool. Their sheaves of compound, feather-like leaves on
tall, thick trunks break up the skyline over the perimeter colonnades. These palms, date-producing
natives of the Middle East, may seem unexpectedly exotic in an otherwise cool Mediterranean-style
planting. However, their use in the Getty Villa garden is historically justified: date palms are depicted
in a wall painting from the House of the Golden Bracelet in Pompeii, indicating that the Romans had
imported them for cultivation already by the first century A.D.

Next along the paths, and opposite the third fountain jet, is a matching pair of woven latticework alcoves, one on either side of the pool. Made of milled cedarwood treated with a special gray
antiquing stain, their arched frames shelter cast-concrete seats, as usual painted Pompeian red.
Travertine drinking fountains here provide visitors with an important amenity in a warm climate.
The side walls of the alcoves provide an attractive foil for bronze busts on white marble posts, like
others throughout the gardens.

The four latticework alcoves are set amid beds of roses, comprising half of the eight
rose beds overall in the Outer Peristyle Garden. They are filled with damask roses, a species that
originated in the eastern Mediterranean region and derives its name from the city of Damascus in

present-day Syria. This strain, the 'Autumn Damask' rose, continues its flowering through the fall, unlike the usual damask rose. Multi-stemmed and pink-flowered, it is here loosely pruned for a natural effect. Its subtle perfume is a bonus, a reminder that it is from the petals of this rose that traditional rose oils are distilled. Being of ancient origin, this rose is a fitting choice for this garden.

The end of the garden farthest from the Villa is dominated by a pair of multi-stemmed European fan palms, one on each side of the garden, which were already seventy-five years old when they were planted in the 1970s. Usually described as "dwarf," they rarely grow to the size of the two specimens here. Natives of southern Europe, they are especially prolific in southern Italy, which makes them appropriate in this context.

Single pink oleanders, also native to southern Italy, have been planted in a loose group around the fan palms. Lurking in their midst are two lifelike bronze figures of boy athletes, one on the north side and one on the south. They hold similar dynamic poses: eyes forward, poised for

action, as if they were about to start a footrace. Their unexpected placement here adds a touch of whimsy to this end of the garden. Classical-style sculpture is rarely seen in today's gardens, so the statues' appearance here provides a rare opportunity for visitors to see and appreciate such works of art in a garden setting.

Located between the European fan palms and at the focal point of this end of the garden is a life-size bronze figure of Hermes (Roman Mercury), the ancient Greek messenger of the gods. Like the other figures in the garden, it was cast by the Chiurazzi foundry after a figure found in the Villa dei Papiri. The figure wears winged sandals, the straps of which are fastened on the soles of his feet by rosettes; being a god, he had no need to tread on the ground. Hermes looks as if he has temporarily come to rest on a rock that consists of two separate blocks of rough-cut travertine, which are surrounded by a swath of large-leaved butcher's broom. The entire composition sits within a circle of Roman bricks laid on edge and set in contrasting beige grout, creating a striking radial pattern around a central rosette.

The range of flower colors used in the Outer Peristyle Garden is less restrained than in the other, smaller gardens of the Villa and includes some bright reds, vibrant oranges, and bold magentas. In early spring, the bright red flowers of the windflower, or anemone, a Mediterranean meadow flower, emerge. In late spring, three different species of bellflower bloom. The ground-covering Serbian bellflower, the taller peach-leaved bellflower, and the even taller and scented chimney bellflower, which sometimes reaches five feet in height, can be distinguished. The nectar-rich lavender-blue flowers of the small scabious attract a variety of pollinating insects. Drifts of rose campion, with its silver leaves and magenta flowers, and of yarrow and ox-eye daisy, both with yellow flowers, brighten the beds in summer. Marigolds, with their orange flowers; mulleins, with their pale yellow flowers; as well as toadflax and iris, both with purple flowers, add their color. Serpentine "rivulets" of violets flow through and between the taller flowers.

The beds are divided into distinct areas of annuals and perennials by sunken redwood headers, as they are in the Inner Peristyle Garden and the East Garden. Among the flowering bulbs are paper-white narcissi, which flower in extensive clumps in winter. Their multiple flower heads, with double ranks of petals, pleasantly scent the areas around them. The Lady tulip, a native of Uzbekistan, colonizes some of the beds, offering its white, star-like flowers in early spring. As it is a wild tulip rather than a highly bred hybrid, its flowers are subtle and delicate rather than showy. The rose-pink flowers of cyclamen pop up in large drifts during the autumn. The loosely flowing planting design of some of the large beds is bolstered visually at intervals by short dwarf hedges of germander and small-leaved ruscus.

This overall diversity of planting and decoration is displayed against a neutral green background provided by two rows of large, standard bay laurel trees, numbering fourteen on either side of the garden. Their regular rhythm corresponds to that of the columns behind them. Like the bay laurels in the other gardens, these are clipped three times a year to maintain their shape and size.

Mr. Getty is on record as worrying that they would obscure the colonnade if they were allowed to get out of hand. Underneath the laurels, gravel paths wind their way around each successive tree. The winding paths are edged on both sides with dwarf hedges of boxwood, which form serpentine lines stretching from one end of the garden to the other. Behind the boxwood hedges, low-clipped domes of rosemary alternate with dwarf myrtle domes along the length of the beds.

The climax of the Outer Peristyle Garden is the view out to the Pacific Ocean. The ocean is visible from the end of the garden through an open Corinthian colonnade backed by a serene grove of mature California sycamores. The preservation of these old native tree specimens was such a high priority that, during the planning of the Villa, the Outer Peristyle Garden was actually scaled back from its originally intended size in order to preserve them. Over the years the original grove has been augmented by new, young trees so that one of the joys of the garden is to pause momentarily here and listen to the wind rustling in their large, palmate leaves. Looking back from this point toward the Villa, it is also possible to appreciate the site's dramatic backdrop, the natural majesty of the Santa Monica Mountains.

The Outer Peristyle Garden of the Getty Villa is a synthesis of architecture, art, and garden. The apparent simplicity of the garden's plan is diversified by the many and varied arrangements of plantings, architectural ornament, and statuary. The controlled richness of its design and its precise maintenance make it an exemplary exercise in archaeological garden reconstruction, ensuring it an iconic place among the gardens of the twentieth century.

Acanthus mollis
BEAR'S BREECH
4–5 ft. (Southwestern Europe,
northwestern Africa)

The leaves and flowers of this plant were the obvious inspiration for the capitals of the Corinthian columns of the Outer Peristyle and part of the ceiling coffers throughout the Villa. Legend has it that in the fifth century B.C., the Greek sculptor Callimachus saw this plant in a cemetery in Corinth and reproduced it in stone as an architectural motif. Its crushed leaves were once used for burns and scalds. If the flower stalks are removed as they emerge, the plant will continue to grow vegetatively through the summer. If left to flower, the plant goes dormant until fall. It prefers a shady location but will grow in full sun. Plant in moist, well-drained loam. Hardy to about 10°.

Achillea tomentosa 'Maynard's Gold'
(or *A. tomentosa* 'Aurea')
WOOLLY YARROW
8 in. (Southern Europe to western Asia)

WOOLLY YARROW is part of the meadow mixture of flowers found throughout Europe. The genus *Achillea* is named for Achilles, the hero of the Trojan War. According to Homer's *Iliad*, the Greeks used YARROW to treat battle wounds. It is an astringent and helps to clot blood. This tight little ground cover is used as a bulb cover when the NARCISSI are finished blooming around the Outer Peristyle pool. After the blooming period, the beds are patched by root divisions of the YARROW. It grows in a wide range of light levels but will flower best in full sun. Likes light, well-drained soil. Hardy to about −20°.

Anemone coronaria
WINDFLOWER
12–18 in. (Mediterranean Basin)

This plant is called WINDFLOWER because the genus name is related to the Greek word *anemos*, or "wind." Legend held that the flowers only open when the wind blows. In Greek mythology, the plant is associated with Aphrodite's lover, Adonis. When he was killed by a wild boar, Aphrodite wept as many tears as Adonis shed drops of blood. Where her tears fell, up sprang a white rose, and where his blood fell, a red anemone grew. These flowers are very common in Greece, where the myth evolved. They are also available in white or purple. At the Villa, they bloom in February. Must have full to partial sun and prefers sandy loam. Hardy to about 30°.

Arbutus unedo
STRAWBERRY TREE
To 25 ft. (Southern Europe, Turkey, Lebanon)

This tree is named for its colorful fruit, which is edible. The botanical name is ancient, and Dioscorides described the plant, but it wasn't especially popular in Roman times. It responds to directional pruning, which makes it a great choice for topiary hedges or vertical screens. The wood is used in wood turning and marquetry, and the bark has been employed in tanning. The fruit is utilized to flavor cordials, and the Romans made marmalade from it, with honey as sweetener. It is native to damp woodlands and likes humic, well-drained soil. It prefers filtered light, which produces sweeter fruit, but it can tolerate full sun. Hardy to about 10°.

Buxus microphylla koreana 'Winter Gem'
WINTER GEM BOXWOOD
5 ft. (China)

The Romans had a similar boxwood, *Buxus sem-pervirens*, and pruned the plants in straight lines or topiary forms, like the hedges and domes at the Getty Villa. This species was chosen due to its more vigorous growth and better suitability for the full sun in Malibu. Ancient gardeners, in addition to planting BOXWOOD in their gardens, harvested mature shrubs from European forests for the wood, which is twice as hard as OAK and excellent for carving and making boxes. There is almost a mile of BOXWOOD hedging in the Outer Peristyle Garden. Plant in full sun to partial shade in any fertile, well-drained soil. Hardy to about −20°.

Calendula officinalis
CALENDULA (or POT MARIGOLD)
To 24 in. (Southern Europe, North Africa)

This bright orange favorite, native to the Mediterranean, can be seen blooming in the Villa gardens year-round. Its botanical name comes from the Latin *calends*, or "throughout the months." The plant produces interesting sickle-shaped seeds and reseeds easily. POT MARIGOLD has many culinary, medicinal, and utilitarian purposes. Petals can be used instead of saffron to add color to salads and eggs. A tea made from the flowers is used for inflammation and as an antiseptic. POT MARIGOLD flowers are added to chicken feed to produce darker yellow yolks, and oil from the seeds is used in soap production. This plant thrives in full sun in well-drained, moderately fertile soil. Annual.

Campanula persicifolia
PEACH-LEAVED BELLFLOWER
To 36 in. (Higher elevations in southern Europe,
central and southern Russia)

This BELLFLOWER prefers a cold period, as it is
native to the Alps and to elevations above 3,000 ft.
in southern Europe. In northern regions, it occurs
at lower elevations. It begins to bloom in June and
will continue through the fall with regular water.
Although it tolerates a fair amount of drought, it
will stop blooming if offered only seasonal rain.
This plant reseeds readily in gravel and can bloom
in blue or white. It tolerates a wide range of light
conditions but flowers best with at least a few
hours of full sun. At the Villa, BELLFLOWERS can
be seen in the Inner Peristyle Garden, but they
bloom longer in the better light of the Outer Peristyle. Prefers alkaline, well drained soil. Hardy to
about −30°.

Chamaerops humilis
EUROPEAN FAN PALM
To 10 ft. (Mediterranean region)

This is the only PALM now native to continental
Europe. It is used as a street tree in Monaco and in
towns along the French Riviera. The EUROPEAN
FAN PALMS in the Outer Peristyle Garden have
an extra 3 ft. of soil in raised concrete planters to
accommodate their roots. The trees were purchased
from residential settings in Southern California
and brought to the Villa in 1974. This PALM is very
durable and tolerates infrequent watering. The
roots are not as aggressive as those of other palms
and grow very slowly. This tree is a good selection
for confined spaces, as it can be maintained in a
small area for many years. But beware the hooks on
the petioles! Situate in full sun to partial shade in
well-drained, moderately fertile to poor soil. Hardy
to about 20°.

Chrysanthemum coronarium
GARLAND CHRYSANTHEMUM
To 32 in. (Mediterranean Basin)

The colorful flowers of this plant contain certain insect-repellent compounds used in insecticides today. This, however, does not stop bees, butterflies, and moths from collecting the pollen. GARLAND CHRYSANTHEMUM blooms from spring through summer. The foliage is often included in Asian recipes. In the fall the plants are cut back to the base for the winter, and in the spring new growth sprouts from the crown. Hardy to about 20°.

Convolvulus sabatius (C. mauritanicus)
GROUND MORNING GLORY
To 24 in. (Spain, Italy, North Africa)

This drought-tolerant perennial is native to coastal locations throughout the Mediterranean. It spreads along the ground from a central crown but does not become invasive. It blooms all year in the coastal climate and requires very little care. This plant will tolerate shade but will not bloom and may become susceptible to thrips because it is stressed. It makes a great hanging-basket plant due to its cascading vines. GROUND MORNING GLORY can be propagated by stem cuttings. It thrives in poor, alkaline, gritty soils with plenty of sun. Hardy to about 20°.

Erysimum cheiri (or *Cheiranthus cheiri*)
WALLFLOWER
18–32 in. (Southern Europe)

This plant lasts for several years and reseeds readily. It grows on untended land throughout Europe
and produces flowers ranging in color from yellow
to red. WALLFLOWERS have reseeded themselves
in the Outer Peristyle Garden in the sunny beds.
They require very little water if mulched and are an
excellent choice to provide color through most of
the year. They flourish on old, sun-drenched walls
with only seasonal water throughout the Mediterranean. Modern selections with large flowers and
new colors are less vigorous and need regular water
and fertilizer. Plant in full sun. Likes poor, alkaline, well-drained soil. Hardy to about −10°.

Iris germanica 'Florentina'
WHITE IRIS
18–20 in. (Mediterranean region)

This is a close relative of the GERMAN IRIS, the
only difference being the flower color. Theophrastus described a ritual in which honey water
was sprinkled on the rhizomes of this flower three
months before harvesting to improve yield, and
Pliny the Elder later described this rite in greater
detail. The roots are dried and powdered to produce
orris root, a prized violet-scented commodity used
in the perfume industry in ancient times as well
as today and a key ingredient in "sapphire" gin.
Orris root is also used in many Moroccan dishes.
WHITE IRIS tolerates most soils but blooms best
in a rocky, sunny site with dry, well-drained soil.
Hardy to about −10°.

Iris germanica
GERMAN IRIS (or BEARDED IRIS)
6–36 in. (Eurasia)

The ancients flavored their wine with the scented roots of this flower. They also extracted oil from the roots to use as a deodorant. In Greek mythology, Iris was the goddess of the rainbow and messenger of Zeus and Hera. These flowers are extremely durable and can withstand severe drought. They should be planted so that the fleshy portion of their roots is on the soil surface, with the tops exposed to the sun. Ample sun on the roots will ensure carbohydrate production and available energy for flowering. GERMAN IRIS is very cold tolerant and survives in northern climates. Needs full sun and well-drained, sandy soil. Hardy to about −10°.

Laurus nobilis
GRECIAN BAY LAUREL
To 40 ft. (Mediterranean region)

Daphne, a nymph beloved by Apollo, was turned into a LAUREL tree to escape his embraces. Hence, the tree was sacred to Apollo, god of healing, and his sanctuary was constructed of its boughs. The BAY LAUREL was associated with victory and peace, and crowns of its leaves were worn by victors of athletic contests and political struggles alike. It was grown in the Roman garden for shade, as described by Pliny the Younger, and was used to flavor roasts, for several medicinal purposes, and for making garlands for Saturnalia and other festivals. The English word *laureate* means "crowned with laurel," appropriate for poets and others favored by Apollo. Plant in full sun to partial shade in fertile, well-drained soil. Hardy to about 20°.

Lilium candidum
MADONNA LILY
To 6 ft. (The Balkans, western Asia)

This elegant garden favorite blooms in the summer. The WHITE LILY motif appears in wall paintings as early as in Minoan times. Homer described
the skin of the warrior Ajax as being "delicate as
a LILY." In Greek mythology, the goddess Persephone was picking meadow flowers including LIL-
IES when she was abducted by Hades, god of the
Underworld. The Romans, too, used the WHITE
LILY to adorn their walls and gardens. The Christian tradition continued to associate it with purity;
like the ROSE, it became a flower emblematic of the
Virgin Mary. In recent times, it has been popular
during the Easter season. Plant in full sun to partial
shade. It likes moist, acidic soil enriched with leaf
mold. Hardy to about 20°.

Linaria purpurea
TOADFLAX
To 36 in. (Southern Europe)

This perennial is native to Italy, where it blooms
a light blue in late spring as part of a European
meadow mix. The genus name means "resem-
bling *linum*" (flax), referring to the long, tapering
leaves. Both plants bloom at the same time in the
dry meadows of Italy. TOADFLAX is toxic to livestock and hence considered a weed by most farm-
ers. It is used medicinally as a strong laxative and
diuretic. This plant has reseeded itself on both
sides of the Outer Peristyle Garden where the light
is filtered and the soil is sandy. It is a favorite of
butterflies and moths when in bloom. Plant in fertile, sandy soil in full sun to partial shade. Hardy to
about −20°.

Lychnis coronaria
ROSE CAMPION
To 30 in. (Southeastern Europe)

The genus name for this plant has persisted since Roman times, when Dioscorides described it as being a key part of a sacrificial wreath. The thick leaves were used as a bandage to hold ointments on open wounds. The bright red flowers continue from spring through fall, when they must be cut back to the basal foliage for the winter season. The seeds are prolific through the summer and can be collected and germinated easily. A white variety is often seen as well. This plant prefers full sun for longest flowering but will bloom even in partial sun. It does best in moderately fertile, well-drained soil. Hardy to about −20°.

Myrtus communis 'Boetica'
MYRTLE
To 10 ft. (Mediterranean)

This aromatic plant was sacred to Aphrodite, goddess of love, who rose from the sea at Paphos on Cyprus and hid her naked beauty behind a MYRTLE plant. It was associated with youth and beauty and was often used to adorn sanctuaries and temples. Theophrastus described this plant in detail, and Dioscorides prescribed the juice of the cooked berries, mixed with wine, for intestinal inflammation. Today it is used in this manner for indigestion. The juice of the blue berries and a decoction of the leaves were used as a black hair dye. It was a prized plant for topiary forms as well. Likes full sun but will tolerate partial shade. Plant in moderately fertile, well-drained soil. Hardy to about 20°.

Narcissus sp. 'King Alfred'
DAFFODIL
18–24 in. (Eurasia)

The genus name for this plant comes from the Greek myth of Narcissus, a youth who fell in love with his own reflection in a pool and pined away with longing. The flowers sprang up at the spot where he died. NARCISSUS was used by the Roman physician Aulus Cornelius Celsus as an ingredient in an emollient and erodent. DAFFODILS are part of the genus *Narcissus*; however, the first are single flowers, while the second have multiple flowers on a single stem. The bulbs have been collected in the wild for centuries and are therefore not as common in Europe as before. They have naturalized in other parts of the world. Grows best in full sun, in moist, well-drained soil. Hardy to about 20°.

Narcissus papyraceus
PAPER WHITES
18–24 in. (Central and western Mediterranean)

These fragrant favorites are named for their thin, papery flowers. They are native to Europe and bloom naturally in the early spring. At the Villa, 5,000 bulbs are timed and planted to bloom during the latter part of December, close to the festivities surrounding Saturnalia and our present-day Christmas season. They are removed after blooming because, though they will naturalize, they need proper chilling to bloom ebulliently each year. Each stem can produce up to 20 flowers. Bulbs can be forced in water. Full sun will produce short, strong leaves that stand up through the blooming period. Plant in fertile, well-drained soil. Hardy to about 20°.

Nerium oleander
OLEANDER
To 20 ft. (Eastern Mediterranean
to western China)

OLEANDER is a very poisonous plant containing many toxic compounds. Pliny the Elder wrote in his *Natural History* that OLEANDER could be used to treat snakebite "if taken in wine with rue." It is planted throughout southern temperate regions due to its adaptability and colorful display. It can tolerate heat and drought, so it has been planted along highways throughout California. It is also a favorite landscape plant for deer-resistant gardening. This plant responds well when the entire shrub is cut back to the crown. The larvae of the common crow butterfly feed on OLEANDER and become unpalatable to predators. Needs full sun but will tolerate a wide range of soil conditions. Hardy to about 20°.

Phoenix dactylifera
DATE PALM
To 100 ft. (North Africa, western Asia)

DATE PALMS have been cultivated for their fruit since recorded history. Their origin is unknown but was probably a desert oasis environment. Images of DATE PALMS appear in wall paintings from every culture in the Mediterranean region. Theophrastus wrote about *Phoenix theophrasti*, the closely related Cretan species named after him. Dates have been used to make wine since antiquity. Ancient cultures wove PALM fronds to make baskets. In California, DATE PALMS bloom and fruit best in Indio, a hot inland city that produces much of the U.S. date crop. On the coast where it is cooler, the trees do not produce fruit. Must have full sun and sandy, well-drained soil. Hardy to about 30°.

Platanus racemosa
CALIFORNIA SYCAMORE
To 80 ft. (Southern California, Mexico)

These beautiful trees, which stand south of the
Outer Peristyle Garden, predate the Villa. They
thrive in moist, sheltered canyons throughout California. The natural spring along the entrance road
provides ample water for these streamside giants.
The stone pits surrounding their bases were built
to allow space for the original crowns of the trees
to have access to air. The naturally occurring pests
of these trees—lace bug, anthracnose, and powdery mildew—appear in the summer months and
can be seen on the leaves as mottled yellowing. If
these pests appear early in the season, the tree has
a chance to defend itself by replacing the damaged
leaves with new growth. If they appear late in the
season, the tree simply goes dormant, because there
is not enough water in the soil to sustain growth.
CALIFORNIA SYCAMORE likes full sun and moist,
humic soil. Hardy to about 10°.

Punica granatum
POMEGRANATE
To 20 ft. (Southern Europe to the Himalayas)

This fruit tree originated on the Iranian plateau and spread through the many civilizations in the region. POMEGRANATE, affiliated with several gods in the ancient world, held a prominent position in Greek mythology. Persephone, daughter of Demeter, was abducted by Hades, ruler of the Underworld. Zeus commanded Hades to release her, but Persephone had already eaten seeds of the POMEGRANATE offered to her by Hades. This compelled her to return to Hades and the Underworld for part of every year; her coming and going was used to explain the change of seasons. The plant's genus name hasn't changed since Roman times. The juice is used as a pigment as well as a delicious drink. Needs full sun and fertile, light soil. Hardy to about 10°.

Rosa 'Autumn Damask'
DAMASK ROSE
4–5 ft. (Middle East)

The most fragrant rose from antiquity, this species has been cultivated for thousands of years for
its aroma. The Romans sprinkled rose petals on
their banquet tables. This notion was the inspiration for the ceiling painting on the West Porch of
the Museum. The DAMASK ROSE has been highly
prized by the perfume industry in France and elsewhere for centuries. The ROSE has many medicinal
uses. The Romans made tea from ripe rose hips to
help sore throat and fever. Today we know that rose
hips contain a high concentration of vitamin C. The
DAMASK ROSE blooms in the spring and intermit-
tently through the rest of the season. Plant in full
sun in fertile, moist, well-drained soil. Hardy to
about −10°.

Rosmarinus officinalis 'Tuscan Blue'
TUSCAN BLUE ROSEMARY
To 5 ft. (Mediterranean region)

The genus name for this herb, which means "dew of
the sea," is an apt one for a coastal plant dedicated
to Aphrodite (Roman Venus), goddess of love, who
rose from the sea. In Roman wedding ceremonies,
the bridegroom had to appear bearing ROSEMARY
in order to establish his dominion over the household. Pliny described ROSEMARY as a plant used
in making head wreaths, and Horace praised it as
an appropriate offering to household gods. At the
Villa, it grows in two forms: an upright hedge form
and a prostrate creeper (*Rosmarinus officinalis*
'Prostratos') that cascades over the walls of the olive
terrace. Must have full sun and prefers dry, alkaline, sandy soil. Hardy to about 20°.

Tulipa clusiana
LADY TULIP
10–12 in. (Iran to the Himalayas)

This elegant flower blooms in the earliest months of the year when the days are shortest. Tulips in every color were described as cloaking the hills when Zeus and Hera were married. Some 5,000 bulbs of this species are planted each year throughout the Villa. This species is from the mountains of eastern Europe, a region much colder than Malibu. Before shipping, the bulbs must be chilled for several months to approximate a normal mountain winter, to ensure that the bulbs sprout as desired. The bulbs are edible, but the ancients appreciated the flowers as a cherished spring sight. Plant in full sun in sandy, well-drained soil. Hardy to about −30°.

Verbascum thapsus
NETTLE-LEAVED MULLEIN
To 5 ft. (Eurasia)

The tall flower spikes of MULLEIN provide a colorful backdrop for the herms in the Outer Peristyle Garden. This plant thrives in full sun, where it produces a multi-stem flower stalk with many flowers, which are a favorite of bees. The perfectly round seed capsules contain hundreds of seeds, which is partially why this plant is considered an invasive weed in much of the western United States. Today MULLEIN is used medicinally as and infusion for bronchitis and to curb mucus production. It is very drought tolerant and blooms in the warm months. Dry, sandy, alkaline soil is best. Hardy to about −10°.

Vitis vinifera 'Perlette'
PERLETTE GRAPE
Vine (Garden origin)

GRAPES have been cultivated for juice and wine since before recorded history. The domesticated vine originated in southwestern Asia around 3500 B.C. In Greek mythology, the grapevine was sacred to Dionysos, god of wine, whom the Romans called Bacchus. The Greeks took up wine-making during the Minoan Age, and Homer refers to it often in his epic poems. Sap from the vine has been used to treat skin diseases. Grape-seed extract is added to antiaging formulas for its antioxidant properties. GRAPES thrive in full sun with moist, fertile, well-drained soil. Hardy to about 10°.

THE HERB GARDEN

Karl Weber noted an area next to the Villa dei Papiri that he believed had been devoted to the production of grapes, olives, and cereals. The Herb Garden at the Getty Villa is conceived as a similar type of garden, one that produces the types of grapes, olives, vegetables, and herbs that the Romans cultivated during the first century A.D. Of the approximately fifty different plants in the garden's many beds, most were used in the kitchen, but some may have had medicinal or religious uses. Many of the plants are aromatic, producing the garden's distinctive ambience.

Visitors may descend into the garden from the forecourt of the Villa, passing on their way a monumental stone pine tree on a high terrace. This tree was already several decades old when it was planted there in 1974. Its spreading, dome-like canopy shades and protects this end of the garden. Below the pine is a low terrace wall constructed in what the ancient Romans called *opus reticulatum* (network), a decorative wall-building technique in which the square-cut stones are set on a diagonal rather than a horizontal line. A blind arch, set in the wall, is constructed of narrow Roman-style bricks alternating with pieces of buff sandstone imported from Gallipoli, Italy. Set in the brickwork beneath the arch is a life-size bronze lion mask, from which water falls into a semi-circular pool. Beds with clumps of scented paper-white narcissi and the sedge- or rush-like papyrus flank the fountain and its pool.

The design of the lower garden revolves around a central "dipping pool." In antiquity, such pools provided a convenient reservoir from which gardeners could fetch water to irrigate the plants. The dipping pool in the Getty Villa is lined with white-veined black marble. A plinth at one end of the pool provides a base for a bronze statuette of a Silenus. This woodland deity, traditionally portrayed as an old man, rides a bulging wineskin whose neck forms a spout from which water plunges into the pool below. Like other statuary in the gardens, the bronze figure was cast by the Chiurazzi foundry and is a copy of one found in the Villa dei Papiri. The pool is decorated with water lilies and papyrus (*Cyperus papyrus*), with its tall, grass-like stems and whorls of fine, greenish brown flowers. Plants of the papyrus family were used in antiquity to manufacture the writing material of that name. Multi-stemmed olive trees, lemon trees, and low cylinders of clipped bay laurel stand sentinel around the pool. Rosemary hedges frame beds of lavender and Roman chamomile, edged with germander.

Two veteran pomegranate trees stand on either side of the garden's central walkway. The pomegranate, though native to Iran, has been cultivated and naturalized around the whole of the Mediterranean since ancient times. These specimens are multi-stemmed and pruned into a goblet shape, like the similar pair in the Outer Peristyle Garden. The picturesquely gnarled and excoriated trunks are underplanted with aromatic lemon balm. The pale yellow fall foliage of the trees provides autumn interest to the garden.

The main area of the garden is arranged in two halves around the central pool. Each half is composed of a series of small rectangular beds, all of equal size and arranged symmetrically around a wide central path. The main path is surfaced with exposed aggregate concrete panels made with decomposed granite. The subsidiary paths, because they get only modest foot traffic, are surfaced with sand.

The beds in the near half of the garden are planted with orderly rows of herbs, with numerous individual plants of a single species to a bed. Many of the herbs, being short-lived, must be replanted regularly. At any given time, one may see beds of sage, basil, hyssop, and germander as well as thyme and mint in different varieties. Each of the three beds along the wall of the Villa has a full-grown damson plum, a tree named for its putative city of origin, Damascus in Syria. This tree was imported to ancient Rome and grown in its gardens. Note that the trunks of these trees have unusual "corkscrew" growth forms.

The slope above this half of the garden is conceived as a terraced olive grove reminiscent of those on the Sorrentine Peninsula, south of the Bay of Naples. The walls are constructed of rough fieldstones from the Ojai area, northwest of Los Angeles. Their mortar joints are recessed so that the masonry resembles the dry-stone walls typical of Italian olive orchards. Like the olives planted on the Entry Path, these multi-stemmed trees are of the 'Swan Hill' fruitless variety. Drifts of roses, of red- and pink-flowered valerian and sea pink, and of yellow-flowered yarrow, Spanish broom, sweet broom, and St. John's wort curve between and under the olive trees to complete the picture.

The other half of the garden replicates the half nearest the museum building but with minor changes in design and planting. This half has a similar layout of rectangular herb beds, mirrored across the central path. However, each bed is planted with two herbs, one as edging, and one making up the center. For example, bands of sea pink, candytuft, and alyssum edge interior plantings of costmary, catmint, and sage. In addition, a standard fruit tree is planted in the center of each bed. Pear, apple, fig, and peach trees—the last with spring flowers of intense pink—grow in paired beds along either side of the central path. A further line of fruit trees, including apricots and quinces, grows in the beds abutting the Villa wall. The quince, a tree native to the Caucasus

Mountains, was grown in Roman gardens, as we know from the garden fresco at Empress Livia's villa at Prima Porta, near Rome.

The fruit-tree theme is continued, at the end of the garden, with a matching pair of citron trees. This tree, a relative of the lemon used for medicinal purposes, is known to have been cultivated in ancient Rome, as it appears in a wall painting in the House of the Orchard at Pompeii. The citrons at the Villa are framed within a rosemary hedge, underplanted with groups of bear's breech and violets and backed with a planting of the deep pink, highly fragrant apothecary's rose (*R. gallica officinalis*). This rose derives its name from the fact that its petals, after processing, boast many curative properties.

Along the outer portion of this half of the garden, visitors can stroll under a rustic grape trellis. The vines, of the seedless 'Perlette' variety, are supported on a simple structure made of Italian alder imported from the Amalfi coast. The poles are bound together with the flexible young shoots of the grapevine in the traditional manner. Cast-concrete seats, painted in Pompeian red, are set within the dappled shade of the overhead vines. Businesslike rows of herbs, such as lovage and chives, and flowers, such as blue flag iris, Moroccan morning glory, and heronsbill, grow in the interior of the beds below. The beds are edged with a variety of flowers, such as borage, with vivid blue blossoms; chamomile, with daisy-like blooms; and wallflowers and cranesbills of many colors.

The grape arbor extends up an adjoining slope to create a visual link between the planting of the Herb Garden and that of the slope. Here the ground is not terraced as it is on the other slope but has been left in its natural landform. It is planted with exotic trees as well as Mediterranean varieties. Two tall date palms, their sheaves of foliage silhouetted against the sky, and long-needled Canary Island pines mix in with more usual Mediterranean trees such as the cork oak and medlars. The last, with their unusual fruit, were historically very common but are now quite rare. Mediterranean shrubs such as oleander, rosemary, and periwinkle are planted among the trees. The planting here is loose in form and arrangement, contrasting with the formal planting in the herb beds below.

At the end farthest from the museum building, an open colonnade connects to the one that terminates the adjoining Outer Peristyle Garden. From its arched balustrade, visitors are treated to climactic views that open up from the garden through the trees of the canyon toward the Pacific Ocean in the distance. The stunning visual experience is enhanced by the whisper of sea breezes through the nearby pines.

Achillea 'Moonshine'
'MOONSHINE' YARROW
24–30 in. (Garden origin)

The astringent and blood-clotting properties of this genus were known to the Romans. As their empire expanded, they found YARROW growing throughout Europe and made consistent use of it. The plant is very drought tolerant and fairly traffic hardy, so it serves as an excellent lawn substitute. It needs to be cut down or mowed twice a season to keep it tidy. The fernlike foliage resembles turf and is aromatic when crushed underfoot. YARROW can be steeped to make a tea to treat fever or combined with PEPPERMINT and ELDER FLOWERS for the early stages of cold or flu. It also lowers blood pressure. Likes full sun to partial shade and rich, well-drained soil. Hardy to about −30°.

Allium schoenoprasum
CHIVES
To 18 in. (Europe, Asia, North America)

This plant is the only member of the ONION family that is native to both Europe and North America. It has been cultivated in gardens since the Middle Ages and long been associated with spring, when the pink flowers make a nice garden show. Dioscorides described the closely related GARLIC as having many medicinal properties. The foliage can be harvested for use in soups, salads, and sauces or as a garnish. The plant is native to cooler regions of Europe and goes through winter as a dormant bulb. CHIVES tolerate a wide range of soil conditions from dry, sandy, alkaline soils to moist, streamside clay. Plant in full sun to partial shade. Hardy to about −30°.

Armeria maritima
SEA PINK
To 12 in. (Europe, Asia Minor, North Africa,
and some coastal North American areas)

This free-flowering plant grows in coastal settings. Dried SEA PINK, harvested in flower, was
traditionally utilized as an antibiotic and to treat
obesity, nervous disorders, and urinary infections.
However, it is rarely employed today, even in folk
medicine. Its best use is as an ornamental edging
in a mixed perennial bed. SEA PINK reached the
height of its popularity in the sixteenth to eighteenth centuries, when it was the premier par-
teere edging choice. It performs best in full sun;
in shade, it will become stressed and susceptible to
thrips. This plant requires regular water and is one
of the first plants to dry out in warm climates. Plant
in poor to moderately fertile sandy soil. Hardy to
about −30°.

Artemisia dracunculus
TARRAGON
12–15 in. (Central and eastern Europe,
southern Russia)

This is one of the most drought-tolerant plants in
the Herb Garden. It survives on very little summer
water and is susceptible to fungal root problems in
wet soil. It has been used as a culinary herb since
antiquity. Today it is associated with French cui-
sine, in which it flavors many sauces for chicken
and fish and herbed butter for lobster. At the Villa,
it rarely produces flowers and is very difficult to
germinate from seed. Therefore, the gardeners
must resort to root division or fresh new plants
if the bed doesn't resprout evenly in the spring.
TARRAGON is cut down to the crown in the fall.
Must have full sun and dry, coarse soil. Hardy to
about −10°.

Borago officinalis
BORAGE
To 24 in. (Europe)

This herb was planted in Roman gardens for its
flowers and attraction for honeybees. Pliny the
Elder described the plant as *Euphrosinum* (mirth)
for its ability to drive away depression—it has
always been associated with merriment. BORAGE
was an ingredient in Pimm's liquor, until it was
replaced with MINT. It is still employed as a garnish for the Pimm's Cup cocktail. The flowers and
leaves have many culinary uses. In Poland, BOR-
AGE leaves are utilized as a pickling spice; Italians
use it as a ravioli stuffing. Medicinally, it is prescribed as an anti-inflammatory and helps regulate
metabolism and hormonal imbalances. Plant in full
sun in any well-drained soil. Annual. Hardy to 20°.

Brassica oleracea
ORNAMENTAL KALE
To 15 in. (Southern Europe to Asia)

This genus has been cultivated for thousands of years. Theophrastus described two domesticated varieties and a wild type in ancient Greece. Today there are hundreds of selections in garden cultivation. Cabbage, broccoli, kale, cauliflower, and the ornamental varieties are all forms descended from an original wild crucifer. This progenitor grows in rocky sites where it tolerates salt and lime, as along the cliffs of Dover in England. It is a cool-season crop in Southern California, where it develops its colorful floret of leaves in the winter and blooms in early spring with a tall spike of yellow flowers. Does well in full sun to partial shade in moist, well-drained soil. Hardy to about 10°.

Capparis spinosa
CAPER
To 18 in. (Mediterranean)

This durable plant is native to the coastal slopes of the Mediterranean and can be seen in abundance along the Amalfi coast in Italy. The genus name hasn't changed in more than 2,000 years. The Romans first developed the process of pickling the unopened flower buds to use as a culinary seasoning. Dioscorides recommended CAPER as a medicinal herb, but the use in sauces dominates its ancient references. The bright-pink stamens and white petals make a striking statement when the flowers are allowed to open. The plant requires very little water and has no pests, making it an excellent choice for dry gardens. Plant in full sun in dry, coarse soil. Hardy to about 30°.

Chamaemelum nobile (or *Anthemis nobilis*)
ROMAN CHAMOMILE
8–12 in. (Europe)

This aromatic herb has been cultivated for millennia. The Romans used the flowers, stems, and roots for various ailments. A mixture made of all plant parts was utilized in a soothing bath to aid with a number of internal maladies, including liver, bladder, kidney, and menstrual problems. A crown of CHAMOMILE was worn to treat a headache. In later times, the Victorians planted this herb on turf benches to make a pleasant place to rest while strolling. The aroma of the crushed foliage was thought to be calming, just as CHAMOMILE tea is today. Grows best in full sun to partial shade in light, well-drained soil. Hardy to about −20°.

Chrysanthemum balsamita
COSTMARY
To 15 in. (Western Europe to western Asia)

This fragrant herb has had many uses since its origin as a meadow plant. Ancient Romans employed it for its medicinal properties. Later it was utilized as an ingredient in brewing ale. It repels silverfish, a destroyer of paper, so for centuries, COSTMARY leaves were used as bookmarks, mainly in books of scripture; thus it came to be called BIBLE PLANT. Its balsam-scented leaves are a sweet addition to potpourris and are used in herbal teas and spring salads. The roots create a dense mat of overlapping rhizomes that will spread over time if not contained or divided. The plant is dormant during the coldest months, sending up fresh new leaves in early spring. Plant in full sun to partial shade in poor to moderately fertile soil. Hardy to about −10°.

Citrus limon
LEMON
15–18 ft. (India)

This modern variety was developed in the twentieth century from plants introduced to ancient Rome during the first century A.D. The original plant came to Europe through Phoenician merchant vessels trading with India, where it was native. The Arabic cultures of the eastern Mediterranean have had access to this plant since Roman times, and the LEMON tree has become typical of Arab-influenced gardens. It has many culinary applications in sauces and beverages. Medicinally, LEMON is used with honey for colds and respiratory ailments. Oil from the peel has astringent properties and is utilized in skin tonics and household cleaners. Needs full sun and moist, well-drained soil. Hardy to about 30°.

Citrus medica 'Etrog'
YELLOW CITRON
12–15 ft. (Southwestern Asia)

This plant is native to Asia, where Alexander the Great led his troops in conquest. He introduced the CITRON to Greece, where it eventually replaced the golden APPLE in the myth of the luxuriant garden of the Hesperides. It was the only citrus fruit in Europe for centuries. The large fruit is not particularly appealing, with meager flesh surrounded by a thick, knobby peel, but the bitter rind has been used as a seasoning since Roman times. The fruit plays a key role in the week-long Jewish festival of *Sukkoth*. Plant in full sun in moist, fertile soil. Hardy to about 30°.

Cydonia oblonga
QUINCE
12–15 ft. (Southwestern Asia)

This small tree is found on rocky slopes in Asia Minor, thriving on scant Mediterranean rainfall. The genus name hasn't changed in 2,000 years, originating on Crete, where the plant was introduced from the Near East. QUINCE was sacred to Aphrodite (Roman Venus), goddess of love, so it was sweetened with honey and eaten at wedding ceremonies in ancient Greece. The flower and fruit from this tree are pictured on ancient coins, often paired with Aphrodite. QUINCE requires full sun to produce the best fruit and likes dry, well-drained soil. Hardy to about −10°.

Cynara cardunculus
CARDOON
To 8 ft. (Southwestern Mediterranean, Morocco)

Theophrastus described this plant, a relative of the THISTLE. Unlike the artichoke, to which it is similar, the stalks of the CARDOON can be eaten. Ancient chefs bound the stalks together and braised them or blanched them in boiling water. CARDOONS were a common garden vegetable for many centuries. They were often planted in colonial American gardens, to be harvested in May, June, and July. Though they fell out of favor in the nineteenth century, they are still cultivated today in parts of Spain and France. CARDOON is a key ingredient in certain cheeses of Portugal and Spain, due to its enzyme content. Plant in full sun. Prefers acidic soil but will grow almost anywhere. Hardy to about 20°.

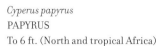

Cyperus papyrus
PAPYRUS
To 6 ft. (North and tropical Africa)

The English word *paper* derives from this species
name, which hasn't changed since ancient Greek
times. The Egyptians harvested PAPYRUS along
the Nile. The stems were peeled and arranged in
crosswise layers, then pounded into a fibrous sheet
to create writing material. The Egyptians, and later
the Romans, ate the stems. Theophrastus described
PAPYRUS as both a vegetable and a utilitarian plant.
Herodotus wrote that its choicest part was the lower
portion, closest to the roots. Ancient peoples used
the fibrous stems to make rope, sandals, baskets,
and even boats. Plant in full sun to partial shade in
a moist, boggy setting. Hardy to about 20°.

Dianthus deltoides
MAIDEN PINK
To 8 in. (Europe and temperate Asia)

The genus name for this plant, which means "flower
of the gods," was bestowed by Theophrastus. Modern cultivars offer many colors, but the original
species color is pink; hence the common name. In
antiquity, PINKS were woven into floral wreaths for
festivals and ceremonies such as weddings, at which
the guests and bridal pair alike wore floral wreaths.
With an aroma similar to cloves, it has long been
a favorite for potpourris. MAIDEN PINK makes a
fine plant for edging or rock gardens. Once established, it can tolerate drying out. Make sure to plant
it in full sun, as shade conditions will stress it and
attract thrips. Likes moist, well-drained soil. Hardy
to about −30°.

Ficus carica 'Black Mission'
BLACK MISSION FIG
To 10 ft. (Eastern Mediterranean)

The FIG has been incorporated into every culture around the Mediterranean. A FIG tree was one of the symbols of fortunate living in many ancient cultures. Athenaeus, an ancient scholar who wrote voluminously about food and wine, devoted a whole chapter to FIGS in his writing. He described a confection prepared with a flour crust and a layer of FIG with honey. Pliny the Elder noted that several varieties had been selected and cultivated in Rome, the best being from Caria in Asia Minor, thus the species name *carica*. Herodotus and Theophrastus both described the complex pollination process, in which gall-wasp-infested fruit from a wild FIG was hung in a domesticated tree. Needs full sun and moist, well-drained soil. Hardy to about 10°.

Geranium macrorrhizum
CRANESBILL
To 15 in. (Southern Europe)

The common name for this plant refers to the shape of its seedpod. CRANESBILL is still used as an aphrodisiac in Bulgaria. The aromatic foliage has been employed in sachets and potpourris since medieval times. It can be seen at the Villa blooming in white or lavender. The flowers are sometimes utilized to decorate cakes. CRANESBILL prefers shade and will make a dense ground cover under trees. It can tolerate a fair amount of sun but will burn during summer months. If mulched, it requires very little water. The plant roots from lateral stems growing along the ground. Plant in moist, well-drained soil. Hardy to about −20°.

Iberis sempervirens
EDGING CANDYTUFT
To 12 in. (Southern Egypt)

According to Greek legend, this plant was part of
the carpet of flowers laid down by the Earth Mother,
Gaia, for the wedding of Zeus and Hera in the garden of the Hesperides. All who attended that festiv-
ity wore wreaths woven with spring flowers such as
this. CANDYTUFT starts blooming in late spring to
early summer and continues into warmer months
if given ample water. It thrives on limestone slopes
and makes a great rock-garden plant. CANDYTUFT
responds well to pruning and can be kept smaller
than its natural size. It blooms best in full sun but
will grow in partial shade. Hardy to about −30°

Lavandula
LAVENDER
24–36 in. (Mediterranean Basin
to Somalia and India)

LAVENDER has had a rich history dating back to
Greek and Egyptian cultures. The name *Lavandula* comes from the Latin *lavare*, "to wash." The
unguents and perfumes buried with King Tut-
ankhamen contained LAVENDER, and the Greeks
anointed their feet with its oil. Theophrastus wrote
about the healing properties of LAVENDER. The
Romans incorporated the flower into wreaths and
garlands and valued the fine honey it produced
when planted near beehives. Dioscorides reported
in his *De materia medica* that LAVENDER taken
internally relieves indigestion, headache, and sore
throat. It was a highly prized scent in ancient Rome,
and a sprig was carried in a pocket to give the aroma
of status to the bearer. The Romans used LAVEN-
DER in their baths to soothe and relax, as is still
done today. Roman women hung it by the bed to
incite passion. LAVENDER is used to flavor beverages and conserves and also in baking to flavor biscuits and cookies. Plant in full sun to partial shade
in dry, gravelly soil. Hardy to about −10°.

(left) Lavandula angustifolia
ENGLISH LAVENDER
Oil from this species is often included in first-aid
kits as a remedy for insect bites.

(center) Dentata
FRENCH LAVENDER
This species is grown as a landscape plant and for
its essential oils, used in the perfume industry.

(right) Stoechas
SPANISH LAVENDER
The Romans named this species after the islands
they called the Stoechades, now the Hyères Islands
off the coast of France near Marseilles. Like ENG-
LISH LAVENDER, SPANISH LAVENDER is used as
an ornamental, with many varying flower sizes and
shades of purple to white.

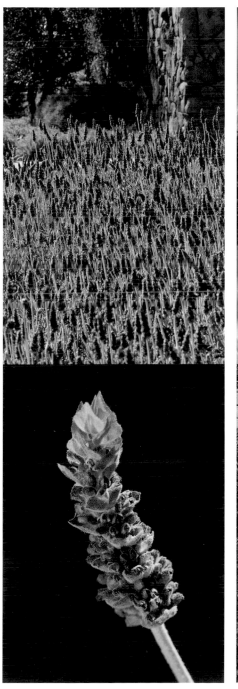

Levisticum officinale
LOVAGE
To 36 in. (Eastern Mediterrnean)

This relative of CELERY has a similar taste and has been used in similar recipes since Roman times. Apicius, an ancient Roman chef, included this herb in at least fifty recipes, usually combining it with pepper. Its flavor is a bit sharper than that of modern CELERY but is quintessentially Roman. Ancient Greeks chewed on the seeds to promote digestion and relieve flatulence. The powdered root was once used like pepper. Young stems of LOVAGE may be candied, fresh leaves are added to soups, and the seeds are added to biscuits and meat dishes. This plant rarely flowers in the Herb Garden. Plant in full sun to partial shade in moist, well-drained soil. Hardy to about −30°.

Linum grandiflorum
CRIMSON FLAX
To 18 in. (North Africa)

This bright flower is one of several FLAX species native to the Mediterranean region and grown at the Villa. This red annual is the most vibrant and easiest to germinate. The pale blue *Linum perenne* is the species used to produce linen. FLAX has been grown for its fibers and seed oil since recorded history. Fabric woven from its stem fibers was used in royal burial garments in ancient Egypt. After weaving, the cloth was bleached with POPPY juice. Homer described FLAX as being used for clothing, sails, and fishing nets. Must have full sun. It is partial to dry, coarse soil. Annual. Hardy to 20°.

Malus pumila (M. domestica) 'Anna'
ANNA APPLE
12–15 ft. (Western Asia)

Wild APPLE trees spread to eastern Europe from western Asia to areas with cold winter frosts. Modern cultivars, such as the ANNA, have been developed to flower and fruit in warmer climates. The APPLE has been cultivated since recorded history and is mentioned in religious texts, often as a forbidden fruit. Alexander the Great sent dwarf APPLE trees back to Greece to his teacher, Aristotle, who studied them as oddities of nature. The APPLE is associated with the Roman goddess of the harvest, Pomona. The culinary uses are endless. Medicinally, it is taken daily to keep the doctor away! Must have full sun to thrive and benefits from rich, well-drained loam. Hardy to about −20°.

Melissa officinalis
LEMON BALM
To 15 in. (Southern Europe)

LEMON BALM was widely planted for its ability to attract honeybees. Indeed, the Latin name for this plant was *apiastrum*, or "bee plant," but it is not the same as BEE BALM (genus *Monarda*). The Romans rubbed this plant on beehives to encourage bees to return. In later times it was steeped in wine and used as a mouthwash. LEMON BALM is used today for a wide range of medicinal applications. A tea made from the leaves relieves stress-related headaches and digestive problems. As a dermal cream, it is used for cold sores or shingles. It thrives in shade as well as sun and responds well to annual pruning to the crown in winter. Hardy to about −20°.

Mentha x piperita
PEPPERMINT
To 12 in. (Europe)

This plant is a cross between WATER MINT, *Mentha aquatic*, and SPEARMINT, *Mentha spicata*. PEPPERMINT was known to the Egyptians, who included it in burial bouquets. According to Pliny the Elder, it was employed for both adornment and flavoring. PEPPERMINT has several medicinal uses. The cooling menthol has been utilized in inhalants and chest rubs for colds and respiratory problems. A tea of its leaves improves digestion and eases nausea. A long-standing custom of serving PEPPERMINT after dinner to freshen the breath still persists. PEPPERMINT oil is used in dental hygiene products and confections such as chocolate. Like other members of the MINT family, it prefers partial sun to shade and moist, well-drained soil. Hardy to about 0°.

Mentha pulegium var. *erecta*
PENNYROYAL MINT
To 4 in. (Central Europe to Iran)

This tight, creeping mint thrives in moist sites that
dry out in summer. It looks dry but is actually dormant until the next rain. Then it flushes with new
growth from the crown. Pliny the Elder described it
and named it *pulegium* for its ability to repel fleas.
PENNYROYAL was later used to sweeten water
stored for long periods aboard ships. It is employed
to make black pudding in northern England and
added to sausage in Spain. Infusions are help-
ful in relieving indigestion, asthma, and painful
menstruation. It can be planted in shady areas as a
lawn substitute. Plant in partial sun to full shade in
moist, rich soil. Hardy to about 10°.

Mentha rotundifolia (or *M. suaveolens*)
APPLE MINT
To 12 in. (Western and southern Europe)

This plant, the most versatile of all the MINTS, can
be grown in sun or shade, indoors or outdoors,
in a container or in the garden. It can be pruned
tight or left to grow naturally. Its woolly leaves
were included in garlands and wreaths in classical
times. As the name suggests, its flavor is a medley
of APPLE and MINT. Today it is used in recipes
with fruit, jellies, sauces, and vinegars. In full sun,
the white flowers attract bees that produce excep-
tional honey from the nectar. If grown indoors, the
tips should be pinched back regularly to promote
branching and keep the plant contained. Plant in
moist, well-drained soil. Hardy to about −20°.

Mentha spicata
SPEARMINT
To 8 in. (Western and central Europe,
Mediterranean)

SPEARMINT was gathered in alpine meadows and
cultivated in gardens to be used in wreaths and garlands. Its fragrant foliage and long-blooming flowers were a favorite for decorating. This MINT was
grown for its healing and culinary uses and as a bee
plant to enhance honey production. The leaves are
utilized to make a tea for indigestion and hiccups.
SPEARMINT is used in beverages such as tea and
mojitos and in Mediterranean dishes such as lamb
tagine and tabbouleh. SPEARMINT oil is employed
in oral hygiene products and chewing gum. Thrives
in partial sun to shade in moist, well-drained soil.
Hardy to about −20°.

Mespilus germanica
MEDLAR
8—10 ft. (Southeastern Europe,
southwestern Asia)

The rarest of all plants at the Villa, this tree comes
from the cold-winter zones of the eastern Mediterranean, where winter chilling comes in the fall
to aid in ripening its fruit. The bottom of the fruit
resembles an APPLE, a close relative. The flower
looks like a ROSE, another close relative. The
Greeks were cultivating this fruit by the second
century B.C. The Romans allowed MEDLAR fruit to
remain on the trees until it "bletted," or ripened
with cold. The fruit becomes soft and sweet and can
be eaten raw, prepared as a jam, or fermented as
wine. Plant in full sun in moist, fertile soil. Hardy
to about −10°.

Nepeta x faassenii
CATMINT
12–15 in. (Garden origin)

This aromatic plant is cherished by cats for its ability to send them into temporary euphoria. It is used
in pet toys and as a dried powder to rub on the carpet. As a landscape plant, its silver foliage and purple flowers through the summer months make it a
fine addition to a perennial border. It doesn't mind
drying out. If planted near the doorway, CATMINT
keeps fleas, mosquitoes, and termites from enter-
ing the house. The oil isolated from this plant also
repels pests but isn't effective if used on the skin.
Plant in full sun in dry, well-drained soil. Hardy to
about −30°.

Nymphaeu sp.
WATER LILY
(Garden origin)

Modern WATER LILY cultivars have been selected
and bred from the wild forms known to Romans
and Egyptians. The wild white variety is native
to rivers and lakes in Europe. Its ancient name,
nenuphar, persisted until the sixteenth century
and comes from Sanskrit via Arabic. Cleopatra had
a blue WATER LILY species in ancient Egypt. The
colorful tropical varieties are Western favorites
but do not tolerate the cold winters of temperate
regions. The LILIES in these areas must be lifted
and replanted or replaced in the spring each year.
They require fertilizer tablets inserted into their
root masses annually. Plant in full sun in ponds
with rich, humic soil. Top with an inch of gravel to
keep the roots in the humic layer. Hardiness varies
by species.

Ucimum basilicum
SWEET BASIL
To 18 in. (Tropical and subtropical Eurasia)

The word BASIL comes from the Greek *basilikon*,
which means "royal." It was considered an imperial herb in antiquity. Pliny the Elder wrote about
the curative effects that the aroma of BASIL has
on fainting spells and headaches. Another Roman
writer, Columella, grew BASIL to flavor his OLIVES
for the table. BASIL lost favor and became associated with evil spirits and sudden death during
medieval times. By the seventeenth century, however, there were fifty varieties recorded. Today
this herb is used fresh in salads, sauces, and as a
garnish. Medicinally, it is used to reduce fever and
tension headaches. It will grow in anything from
full sun to shade in moist, well-drained soil. Hardy
to about 35°.

Olea europaea 'Swan Hill'
SWAN HILL OLIVE®
To 25 ft. (species native to the
Eastern Mediterranean)

The story of the OLIVE tree goes back as far as
recorded history. It was offered to the city of Athens
by its divine protectress, Athena, as a useful gift.
Since the days of ancient Greece, it has been associated with victory and peace. This tree was a source of
Athens's wealth in classical times and was awarded
to victors in the Panathenaic Games. The fruit, oil,
and lumber of the OLIVE had countless applications. The strong wood was utilized to support
mine shafts and galleries in ancient quarries. The
oil was burned for light and employed in cooking
and medicinal preparations. The fruit was soaked
and processed for eating, as is done today. Roman
demand for OLIVE oil was such that vast orchards
had to be cultivated in the fringes of the Empire,
from North Africa to the eastern Mediterranean.
Amphorae filled with OLIVE oil were stacked in
layers in ships bound for Rome from all points in
the growing region. The first pressing of oil went
for cooking, the second for medical applications,
and the third for lamp oil. Today, OLIVE leaves are
steeped in tea to lower blood pressure and relieve
nervous tension. In cooking, OLIVE oil is preferred
to other oils because it is a monounsaturated fat. It
helps the digestive system, circulation, and the skin.
The cultivar grown at the Villa, 'Swan Hill,' is fruitless, which helps reduce the late-summer cleanup;
otherwise, the ripening fruit would stain the walking surfaces and create slip hazards. OLIVES can
be quite drought tolerant but will not produce fruit
without regular water. To withstand dry periods,
OLIVE trees must be grown from saplings in order
to establish extensive root systems. Plant in full sun
in dry, alkaline soil. Hardy to about 20°.

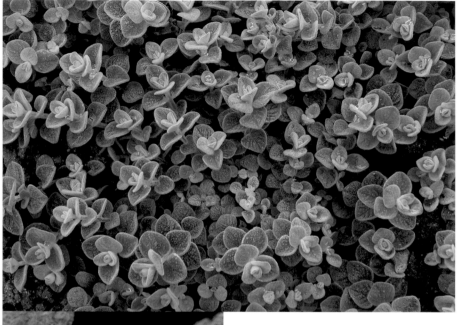

Origanum dictamnus
DITTANY OF CRETE
To 6 in. (Crete)

This plant is native to the mountains on the island of Crete, which were known as the birthplace of Zeus. The plant was incorporated into Greek mythology: the gods ventured to the island to obtain its healing powers. Virgil, Dioscorides, and Pliny the Elder all mention its curative potency. In antiquity, women relied upon DITTANY OF CRETE during childbirth, believing that Artemis, goddess of childbirth, considered this plant sacred. It likes to dry out and makes a nice rock-garden plant. Thrives in full sun in dry, coarse soil. Hardy to about 10°.

Origanum majorana
SWEET MARJORAM
To 12 in. (Southwestern Europe and Turkey)

The pungent aroma of MARJORAM is best appreciated when the small white flowers are emerging from the green buds. Greeks and Romans made garlands and wreaths of it, cooked with it, used it for many medicinal and cosmetic applications, gave it as gifts, and used it in rituals. This plant has been found in many Roman graves in Egypt, suggesting that it had a part in burial ceremonies. Hymen, the god affiliated with marriage, and Amor, the god of love, were said to linger only where MARJORAM bloomed. It was among the top ten cooking herbs found in a Roman garden, used in sauces for cooked meats and to aid digestion. Does best in full sun in poor, alkaline soil. Hardy to about 10°

Origanum vulgare
OREGANO
12–15 in. (Eastern Mediterranean
and temperate Asia)

The generic name for this plant, *Origanum*, comes from Greek and means "joy of the mountain," referring to its pungent aroma and colorful flowers. The highest-quality oregano, grown in its native southern Europe, is strong enough to numb the tongue. The taste is influenced by climate more than by variety and tends to be blander in temperate regions. OREGANO was used in early times as a strewing herb when earthen floors were common. As a medicinal herb, OREGANO has antioxidant activity, and in antiquity, infusions of the herb were prescribed for respiratory problems. As a cooking herb, it has been employed in sauces and with meat in every culture of the Mediterranean Basin. Plant in full sun to partial shade in dry, rocky soil. Hardy to about 10°.

Pinus pinea
ITALIAN STONE PINE (or UMBRELLA PINE)
To 70 ft. (Mediterranean)

The oldest PINE at the Villa was planted in 1974, when it was at least twenty-five years old. STONE PINE is native to coastal regions near the Mediterranean and was associated with Poseidon, god of the sea, due to its widespread use in shipbuilding. Its lumber was used in large quantities to build ships and bridges for military conquests, which meant that vast PINE forests in Greece were destroyed as early as in classical times. Harvesting this tree for its edible seeds, the PINE nuts, has been a common practice for millennia. The hillsides surrounding the Villa have been planted with many STONE PINES, which will eventually tower above the other trees, creating a typical Roman horizon. Must have full sun and dry, well-drained soil. Hardy to about 10°.

Prunus x domestica
PLUM
To 15 ft. (Southern Europe)

The PLUM was described by Dioscorides and was eaten by Romans fresh and in compotes and preserves. PLUM wood was highly prized for fine woodworking. The Romans were the first to use this tree for the practice of pleaching, in which branches of separate trees were bound together to make arches and trellises. Pleaching made artful garden structures and also facilitated fruit gathering. The trunks have a "corkscrew" appearance that occurs naturally and becomes more pronounced with age. PLUM trees can be "dry-farmed" using minimal water, a method that produces the sweetest fruit. Situate in full sun with well-drained soil. Hardy to about −10°.

Prunus persica
PEACH
To 25 ft. (China)

The spring flowers distinguish the three varieties of PEACH growing in the Herb Garden. In order to thrive, most PEACH varieties need more hours of winter chill than is available in Malibu, so each year is a test for these trees. This fruit tree was cultivated by the Chinese as far back as the tenth century B.C. The tree was traded and planted along the Silk Road, before the Roman Empire was thriving around the Mediterranean. Early Greeks thought the PEACH was native to Persia because Alexander the Great brought it to Greece following his conquests there. The species name, *persica*, reflects that belief. Plant in full sun in moist, fertile soil. Hardy to about −10°.

Pyrus communis
EUROPEAN PEAR
To 18 ft. (Southern Europe, southwestern Asia)

This tree was known to the ancient Greeks and was described by Homer in *The Odyssey* as part of the lush, fruitful orchard of King Alcinous. Pliny the Elder described three dozen varieties grown in Roman times. The Romans did not eat the fruit raw but rather stewed it with honey and pepper. PEARS and APPLES are closely related and sometimes look the same in leaf and fruit. One difference is that the flesh of PEARS contains "stone cells," which give the fruit its gritty texture. PEARS are often harvested before they are ripe and left for weeks to ripen. The trees require little water and can thrive in a wide range of soils, given full sun. Hardy to about −20°.

Raphanus sativus
RADISH
To 6 in. (Eurasia)

The generic name for this plant has been Latinized from the Greek but has survived since ancient times. It means "quickly appearing," referring to its 28-day seed-to-harvest crop cycle. RADISH has been prescribed since antiquity as a remedy for liver problems, and Dioscorides wrote of its use as a treatment for skin diseases. He also described RADISH being cooked in ancient Egypt. It helps to promote salivation and digestion and has been enjoyed in salads since antiquity. Crops are often seeded thickly and thinned as they mature, so the remainder of the crop has room to develop. Plant in full sun in moist, sandy soil. Hardy to about 10°. Annual.

Rosa 'Gloria mundi'
GLORIA MUNDI ROSE
To 4 ft. (Garden origin)

This ROSE was bred in the Netherlands in 1929
and has been a garden favorite ever since. It has
very little fragrance, but it is beloved for its showy
clusters of red flowers, which cascade from 10-foot
arching canes. Pliny and Theophrastus described
"sixty-petaled" ROSES not unlike this one. ROSES
can be seen in wall paintings in Pompeii. Blossoms
bound together in garlands and crowns have been
preserved in Graeco-Roman tombs. According to
Greek legend, originally all roses were white, until
Aphrodite pricked herself while rushing to save the
dying Adonis. Drops of her blood fell and dyed the
ROSES red. Needs full sun and plenty of water and
nutrients. Hardy to about 15°.

Rosmarinus officinalis
ROSEMARY
To 4 ft. (Mediterranean region)

The aroma of ROSEMARY was believed to clear the
head when one lingered near it in a garden. It was
burned in temples as an offering to gods. Horace
wrote that if ROSEMARY were offered up, no other
"bloodied beast" was needed to appease the gods.
Due to its aromatic oils, it was often used as a substitute for more costly incense. It was planted near
beehives to improve honey flavor and fermented
with wine as a healthful tonic. Romans did not use
ROSEMARY as a culinary herb but reserved it for
ritual and medicinal purposes. Grows well in full
sun to partial shade and prefers dry, coarse soil.
Hardy to about 15°.

Salvia argentea
SILVER SAGE
To 36 in. (Southern Europe, North Africa)

The hairy, silvery leaves of this plant make it a perfect selection for dry, hot gardens. The hairs insulate and shade the leaves from scorching sun. SAGE
will tolerate drought but prefers regular water to
look its best. It will grow in full shade but will only
flower in full sun. All members of the SAGE family have square stems. These can best be seen when
the plant is in bloom, with white flowers on 18-inch
stalks. This SAGE is another of the bee plants used
by the Romans to enhance honey flavor. In Southern California, it grows best when planted in the
fall. Plant in full sun to partial shade in moist, well-
drained soil. Hardy to about −10°.

Salvia officinalis
CULINARY SAGE
To 24 in. (Mediterranean, North Africa)

Roman herbalists used the genus name *Salvia* solely
for this plant, but today it is shared by many other
plants worldwide. Romans employed the leaves and
stems to produce a tonic used to darken the hair
and give it shine. Pliny the Elder described the use
of this plant in dispelling worms from abscesses
and infected ears. There were many other medicinal applications for this plant, but no evidence
that it was utilized for cooking. Today it is added
to sauces, meat dishes, beans, and potato recipes.
Italians deep-fry the leaves and add them to dishes
as a crunchy garnish. This plant only blooms in full
sun but otherwise tolerates partial shade. Plant in
moist, well-drained soil. Hardy to about 30°.

Stachys byzantina
LAMB'S EAR
To 18 in. (Caucasus to Iran)

The leaves of this plant were used in antiquity to bandage wounds. The woolly surface of the leaves would hold a poultice or salve on a cut when secured in place with cord. LAMB'S EAR grows in poor, gritty soil throughout the eastern Mediterranean, where many battles were fought and wounded soldiers had to seek out herbs to bind their wounds. The plant blooms in late spring with white or pink flowers on very hairy stalks. LAMB'S EAR can tolerate severe drought. It may dry out and die back, but it will re-sprout from the stems when water is available again. The roots form a thick mat over time that will take over if left unchecked. Plant in full sun to partial shade. Prefers dry, sandy, alkaline soil. Hardy to about −20°.

Teucrium chamaedrys (or *Teucrium x lucidrys*)
GERMANDER
To 12 in. (Europe, southwestern Asia)

The Romans called this plant *quercula*, or "little oak," alluding to its foliage. GERMANDER was used in wine as a tonic. It was later utilized in France and England in knot gardens because it could easily be pruned and shaped into hedges. GERMANDER makes a fine edging plant in full sun or partial shade where the pink flowers attract honeybees. The foliage is employed in liqueurs, vermouth, and tonic wines and medicinally as an infusion for gallbladder and digestive disorders. GERMANDER can tolerate minimal water and has no insect pests in modern perennial borders. Plant in full sun to partial shade in moist, well-drained soil. Hardy to about −10°.

Thymus
THYME
2–12 in. (Mediterranean, southwestern Asia)

Ancient Egyptians employed THYME for embalming. The Greeks used it as incense in their temples and associated the plant with courage. Romans planted THYME near their beehives and sold the honey as a specialty item. It was burned to create fumes that were considered antiseptic. Ancient beekeepers would smoke their hives with THYME in the fall to repel vermin. Roman chefs created many flavorful sauces combining full-bodied herbs, including THYME, with fish sauce (*garum*) and oil. This herb is utilized today as in antiquity to flavor soups, stews, and meat dishes. For most uses, the small leaves must be stripped from older, woody stems, but the fresh green tips can be minced stems and all. Hardy to about 0° or colder, depending on the species.

(*left top*) *Thymus pulegioides* 'Bertram Anderson'
LEMON-SCENTED THYME
To 8 in.
This modern THYME selection has a light lemon scent that goes well with seafood and poultry dishes. The leaves can be crushed and applied to the skin as an effective mosquito repellent. The plant can tolerate full sun, if mulched, but prefers some shade. It lasts several years and responds well to harvesting or light pruning. This is a good choice for planting between stepping-stones, where foot traffic releases the citrus fragrance. Prefers moist, well-drained, fertile soil.

(*left bottom*) *Thymus herba-barona*
CARAWAY THYME
To 8 in.
The common name for this plant suggests the flavor similarities to CARAWAY, which this herb can replace in any recipe. This variety derives its species name from the English practice of using it to flavor barons (loin cuts) of beef. The plant is very drought tolerant and can be used between stepping-stones,

where the fragrance is released when trod upon. Plant in full sun in dry, alkaline soil.

(right top) Thymus pseudolanuginosus
WOOLLY THYME
To 4 in.
This THYME has hairy leaves, hence its common name. The Romans planted this cascading ground cover for use in the kitchen and for the pungent honey that bees produced from it. WOOLLY THYME needs a few hours of daily sun to look its best. It is the shortest THYME and can be used as a lawn substitute if partially shaded. It likes dry, sandy soil.

(right middle) Thymus serpyllum
CREEPING THYME (or MOTHER OF THYME)
To 8 in.
Serpyllum was the Latin name for this species 2,000 years ago and refers to its snakelike development. It grows wild on Mount Hymettus near Athens, where the spring blooming period is famous for its display of color. This THYME is the origin of most modern cultivars, for which reason it is sometimes called MOTHER OF THYME. Oil, called *serpolet*, distilled from the stems and leaves, has been promoted in herbal medicine for centuries as a treatment for abscesses and skin ailments. Thrives in full sun in moist, well-drained soil.

(right bottom) Thymus vulgaris
COMMON THYME
To 12 in.
This is the most widely used species of THYME. This herb has antiseptic qualities, and ancient physicians prescribed it for headache and intestinal complaints. Today, the active ingredient, thymol, is employed in expectorants and carminatives. Plant in full sun to partial shade in moist, well-drained soil.

Verbascum bombyciferum 'Arctic Summer'
WOOLLY MULLEIN
To 6 ft. (Turkey)

This plant is quite at home in Southern California, where it gets full sun and only seasonal water. It will tolerate regular water but prefers to dry out for long periods. The thick, felty leaves are covered with dense hairs that shade the leaf surface and insulate the plant from extreme temperatures. The flower stalks can be pinched back to encourage the foliage to persist. Once the flower stalks begin to bloom, they will continue to do so until they set seed and slowly decline. The plant reseeds best in early spring in a sunny, gravelly site with dry, alkaline soil. Annual. Hardy to 10°.

A

acanthus, 39, 60, 84
  Acanthus mollis (bear's breech), 70, 90, 113
Achillea (yarrow), 37, 87, 112
  'Moonshine' ('moonshine' yarrow), 116
  tomentosa 'Maynard's Gold' [*A. tomentosa 'Aurea'*] (woolly
    yarrow), 91
alders, Italian, 38
Allium schoenoprasum (chives), 114, 117
Alocasia veitchii (elephant ear), 40, 42
alyssum, 112
Anemone coronaria (windflower), 87, 92
Anna apple (*Malus pumila* [*M. domestica*] 'Anna'), 112, 131
Anthemis nobilis (*Chamaemelum nobile*; Roman chamomile),
    112, 121
apothecary's rose (*Rosa gallica officinalis*), 113
apple, Anna (*Malus pumila* [*M. domestica*] 'Anna'), 112, 131
apple mint (*Mentha rotundifolia* [*M. suaveolens*]), 133
apricots, 112
arbors
  in Outer Peristyle Garden, 84–85
  in Roman gardens, 12
Arbutus unedo (strawberry tree), 38, 71, 93
architectural and sculptural decoration, in Roman gardens,
    12–13
Armeria maritima (sea pink), 112, 118
arrowhead, 69
Artemisia dracunculus (tarragon), 119
art works, display of in Roman gardens, 11–12. *See also*
    sculpture
Atlantic cedar (*Cedrus atlantica*), 40

B

baby cyclamen (*Cyclamen hederifolium*), 72
baby's tears (*Soleirolia soleirolii*), 67
ballerina musk rose (*Rosa* 'Ballerina'), 53
basil, sweet (*Ocimum basilicum*), 112, 137
bay laurel. *See* Grecian bay laurel
bearded iris (*Iris germanica*; German iris), 98
bear's breech (*Acanthus mollis*), 70, 90, 113
bellflower (*Campanula*), 27, 60
  chimney (*C. pyramidalis*), 63, 87
  Dalmatian (*C. portenschlagiana* [*C. muralis*]), 44
  globe (*Campanula glomerata*), 43
  peach-leaved (*Campanula persicifolia*), 87, 95
  Serbian (*Campanula poscharskyana*), 62, 87
Bellicard, Jérôme-Charles, 61
Bellis perennis (English daisy), 37, 43
benches, 28
bindweed, Moroccan, 37
birdbaths, Inner Peristyle Garden, 61
bird's nest fern, 71
black mission fig (*Ficus carica* 'Black Mission'), 112, 125
blue flag iris, 114
borage (*Borago officinalis*), 114, 119
Boston ivy (*Parthenocissus tricuspidata*), 39, 51
boxwood, 27, 71, 84, 89
  winter gem (*Buxus microphylla koreana* 'Winter Gem'), 94
Brassica oleracea (ornamental kale), 120
broom
  butcher's (*Ruscus aculeatus*), 27, 60, 69, 70, 78, 87
  Spanish, 112
  sweet, 112
buckthorn, Italian, 60, 71, 77

bush morning glory (*Convolvulus cneorum*), 45
butcher's broom (*Ruscus aculeatus*), 27, 60, 69, 70, 78, 87
Buxus microphylla koreana 'Winter Gem' (winter gem
    boxwood), 94

C

Calendula officinalis (calendula; pot marigold), 94
California poppy, 37
California sycamore (*Platanus racemosa*), 37, 89, 104
Campanula (bellflower), 27, 60
  glomerata (globe bellflower), 43
  persicifolia (peach-leaved bellflower), 87, 95
  portenschlagiana [*C. muralis*] (Dalmatian bellflower), 44
  poscharskyana (Serbian bellflower), 62, 87
  pyramidalis (chimney bellflower), 63, 87
Canary Island pine (*Pinus canariensis*), 38, 51, 114
candytuft, edging (*Iberis sempervirens*), 112, 127
caper (*Capparis spinosa*), 120
Capparis spinosa (caper), 120
caraway thyme (*Thymus herba-barona*), 150–151
cardoon (*Cynara cardunculus*), 123
car park, roof and planter plants, 37
Carroll, Maureen, 16–17
caryopteria, 39
catmint (*Nepeta x faassenii*), 112, 136
Cato the Elder, 21
cedar, Atlantic (*Cedrus atlantica*), 40
Cedrus atlantica (Atlantic cedar), 40
Centranthus ruber (Jupiter's beard), 45
Cercis siliquastrum (Judas tree), 38
Chamaemelum nobile (*Anthemis nobilis*; Roman chamomile),
    112, 121
Chamaerops humilis (European fan palm), 27, 38, 86, 95
chamomile, 60, 84, 114
  Roman (*Chamaemelum nobile*; *Anthemis nobilis*), 112, 121
Cheiranthus cheiri (*Erysimum cheiri*; wallflower), 97, 114
chimney bellflower (*Campanula pyramidalis*), 63, 87
Chiurazzi, Gennaro, 28
Chiurazzi Artistic Foundry, 28, 84, 87, 111
chives (*Allium schoenoprasum*), 114, 117
Chrysanthemum
  balsamita (costmary), 112, 121
  coronarium (Garland chrysanthemum), 96
citron, yellow (*Citrus medica* 'Etrog'), 113, 122
Citrus
  limon (lemon), 112, 122
  medica 'Etrog' (yellow citron), 113, 122
climate, 25, 33
coast redwood, 37, 40
Cochin, Charles-Nicolas, 61
color, in Getty Villa gardens, evergreens as source of, 27
columns, in Roman gardens, 11
common thyme (*Thymus vulgaris*), 151
Convolvulus
  cneorum (bush morning glory), 45
  sabatius [*C. mauritanicus*] (ground morning glory), 96
Coreopsis lanceolata (tickseed), 46
cork oak (*Quercus suber*), 38, 52, 114
Corsican hellebore (*Helleborus argutifolius*), 70, 73
Corsican rose. *See* Corsican hellebore
costmary (*Chrysanthemum balsamita*), 112, 121
cranesbill
  Dalmatian, 39
  Geranium-macrorrhizum, 114, 126

creeping jenny (*Lysimachia nummularia*), 60, 66
creeping thyme (*Thymus serpyllum*; mother of thyme), 151
crimson flax (*Linum grandiflorum*), 130
crocus, 27, 70
culinary sage (*Salvia officinalis*), 147
Cupressus sempervirens (Italian cypress), 38, 39, 47
cyclamen, 70, 87
    baby (*C. hederifolium*), 72
Cydonia oblonga (quince), 112–113, 123
Cynara cardunculus (cardoon), 123
Cyperus papyrus (papyrus), 111–112, 124
cypress, Italian (*Cupressus sempervirens*), 38, 39, 47

D

daffodil (*Narcissus sp.* 'King Alfred'), 101
daisy
    English (*Bellis perennis*), 37, 43
    globe (*Globularia meridionalis*), 39, 50
    ox-eye, 87
Dalmatian bellflower (*Campanula portenschlagiana [C. muralis]*), 44
Dalmatian cranesbill, 39
damask rose (*Rosa* 'Autumn Damask'), 85–86, 106
damson plum, 112
date palm (*Phoenix dactylifera*), 103, 114
    in Getty Villa gardens, 85
    in Roman gardens, 18, 85
Dianthus deltoides (maiden pink), 124
Digitalis purpurea (foxglove), 60, 64, 70–71
Dioscorides, 25
Ditta Medici workshop, 61
dittany of Crete (*Origanum dictamnus*), 140
dwarf myrtle, 39, 60, 89

E

East Garden
    map of, 34–35
    plantings and features, overview of, 69–71
    plant species, 72–81
    sculpture, 70
    Villa architecture echoed in, 27
    walls and gates, 69
    water features, 28, 69–70
Echium candicans [E. fastuosum] (pride of Madeira), 39, 48
edging candytuft (*Iberis sempervirens*), 112, 127
elephant ear (*Alocasia veitchii*), 40, 42
Emmet Wemple and Associates, 25
English daisy (*Bellis perennis*), 37, 43
English holly (*Ilex aquifolium*), 70, 74
English ivy (*Hedera helix*), 59, 65, 70, 84
English lavender (*Lavandula angustifolia*), 128–129
entrance driveway, 37
Entry Path, 40
    plantings and features, overview of, 37–40
    plant species, 42–57
    retaining walls, 39
Entry Pavilion, 37
Erodium reichardii [E. chamaedryoides] (heronsbill), 48, 114
Erysimum cheiri (Cheiranthus cheiri); (wallflower), 97, 114
Euphorbia characias wulfenii (spurge), 49
European fan palm (*Chamaerops humilis*), 27, 38, 86, 95
European pear (*Pyrus communis*), 112, 144
evergreens
    in Roman gardens, 16, 18

as source of year-round color, 27
exercise facilities, in Roman gardens, 12

F

fan palm, European (*Chamaerops humilis*), 27, 38, 86, 95
Favret Artistic Mosaics, 70
fences, in Roman gardens, 12–13
fern, bird's nest, 71
fertilizing, guidelines for, 33
feverfew (*Tanacetum parthenium*), 70, 80
Ficus carica 'Black Mission' (black mission fig), 112, 125
fig, black mission (*Ficus carica* 'Black Mission'), 112, 125
flax
    crimson (*Linum grandiflorum*), 130
    toadflax (*Linaria purpurea*), 87
Florentine iris, 84, 97
flowers, in Roman gardens, 20
foliage texture and form, visual interest from, 60
Fonderia Storica Chiurazzi, 28, 84, 87, 111
food gardens, in Roman gardens, 12, 21
fountains. *See* water features
foxglove (*Digitalis purpurea*), 60, 64, 70–71
French lavender (*Lavandula dentata*), 128–129
fruit trees, in Roman gardens, 18, 20–21

G

garden spaces
    in Getty Villa gardens
        scale of, 27
        symmetry of, 27
    in Roman gardens, 11–12
        design principles in, 11
Garland chrysanthemum (*Chrysanthemum coronarium*), 96
Garrett, Stephen, 24
Geranium macrorrhizum (cranesbill), 114, 126
germander (*Teucrium chamaedrys; T. x lucidrys*), 87, 112, 149
German iris (*Iris germanica*; bearded iris), 98
Getty, J. Paul
    and construction of Getty Villa gardens, 29
    and design of Getty Villa, 23, 24–25
    on garden design, 89
    interest in Greek and Roman antiquities, 23
    A Journey from Corinth, 24
Getty Villa
    design of, 23, 24–25
    interplay between interior and exterior spaces, 24
    site of, 24
Getty Villa gardens
    continuity of style throughout, 70, 84
    design of, 25
    map of, 34–35
    Roman model for, 11, 23–24. (*See also* Villa dei Papiri)
Gleason, Kathryn, 16–17
globe bellflower (*Campanula glomerata*), 43
globe daisy (*Globularia meridionalis*), 39, 50
Globularia meridionalis (globe daisy), 39, 50
gloria mundi rose (*Rosa* 'Gloria mundi'), 145
grape hyacinth, 27, 60
grapevines, 27, 85, 114
    perlette grape (*Vitis vinifera* 'Perlette'), 109, 114
grasses, Italian meadow, 39
Grecian bay laurel (*Laurus nobilis*), 27, 59–60, 70, 87–88, 98, 112
green lavender cotton (*Santolina rosmarinifolia [S. virens]*), 54

Greutert, Henry, 84
grottoes. *See* nymphaea
ground morning glory (*Convolvulus sabatius [C. mauritanicus]*), 96

H

Hedera helix (English ivy), 59, 65, 70, 84
hedges
    in East Garden, 70
    in Herb Garden, 113
    in Inner Peristyle Garden, 60
    maintenance of, 27
    in Outer Peristyle Garden, 84, 87, 89
    in Roman gardens, 20
hellebore, 60
    Corsican (*Helleborus argutifolius*), 70, 73
Helleborus argutifolius (Corsican hellebore), 70, 73
Herb Garden
    grape trellis, 114
    map of, 34–35
    olive grove, 112
    plantings and features, overview of, 111–114
    plant species, 116–153
    sculpture, 111–112
    terrace wall, 111
    Villa architecture echoed in, 27
    water features, 28, 111
herms, in Roman gardens, 16
heronsbill (*Erodium reichardii [E.chamaedryoides]*), 48, 114
holly, English (*Ilex aquifolium*), 70, 74
holm oak, 38
House of Livia (Prima Porta), 20, 25
House of Loreius Tiburtinus (Pompeii), 15
House of the Great Fountain (Pompeii), 15, 70
House of the Orchard (Pompeii), 20, 113
House of the Waterjets (Conimbriga, Portugal), 15
hyacinth, grape, 27, 60
hyssop, 112

I

Iberis sempervirens (edging candytuft), 112, 127
Ilex aquifolium (English holly), 70, 74
Inner Peristyle Garden
    birdbaths, 61
    maintenance of, 28–29
    map of, 34–35
    plantings and features, overview of, 59–61
    plant species, 62–67
    sculpture, 59, 60–61
    soil of, 28
    Villa architecture echoed in, 27
    water features, 28, 59, 61
Iris, 27, 70–71, 87
    blue flag, 114
    ensata 'Variegata' (Japanese water iris 'variegata'), 75
    germanica (German iris; bearded iris), 98
    germanica 'Florentina' (white iris), 84, 97
    pseudacorus (yellow flag), 76
    Siberian, 59
    x Louisiana 'Ann Chowning' (louisiana iris), 75
Italian alders, 38
Italian buckthorn, 60, 71, 77
Italian cypress (*Cupressus sempervirens*), 38, 39, 47
Italian meadow grasses, 39

Italian stone pine (*Pinus pinea*; umbrella pine), 27, 38, 111, 142
ivy
    Boston (*Parthenocissus tricuspidata*), 39, 51
    English (*Hedera helix*), 59, 65, 70, 84
    maintenance of, 27

J

Japanese water iris 'variegata' (*Iris ensata* 'Variegata'), 75
Jashemski, Wilhelmina, 16–17, 25
Jerusalem sage, 37, 39
A Journey from Corinth (Getty), 24
Judas tree (*Cercis siliquastrum*), 38
Jupiter's beard (*Centranthus ruber*), 45

K

kale, ornamental (*Brassica oleracea*), 120

L

lady tulip (*Tulipa clusiana*), 87, 107
lamb's ear (*Stachys byzantina*), 148
landscape architect, 25
lanterns, 28
Lathyrus latifolius (perennial pea), 50
laurel, Grecian bay (*Laurus nobilis*), 27, 59–60, 70, 87–88, 98, 112
Laurus nobilis (Grecian bay laurel), 27, 59–60, 70, 87–88, 98, 112
Lavandula. *See* lavender (*Lavandula*)
lavender (*Lavandula*), 39, 112, 128–129
    English (*L. angustifolia*), 128–129
    French (*L. dentata*), 128–129
    Spanish (*L. stoechas*), 128–129
lavender cotton, 39
lemon balm (*Melissa officinalis*), 112, 132
lemon-scented thyme (*Thymus pulegioides* 'Bertram Anderson'), 150
lemon tree (*Citrus limon*), 112, 122
Levisticum officinale (lovage), 114, 130
light fixtures, 28
Lilium Candidum (Madonna lily), 60, 99
lily, 27. *See also* water lily
    Madonna (*Lilium Candidum*), 60, 99
Linaria purpurea (toadflax), 87, 99
Linum grandiflorum (crimson flax), 130
Livia (Empress of Rome), house at Prima Porta, 70, 113
London plane tree (*Platanus x acerifolia* 'Columbia'), 70, 76
louisiana iris (*Iris x Louisiana* 'Ann Chowning'), 75
lovage (*Levisticum officinale*), 114, 130
Lychnis coronaria (rose campion), 87, 100
Lysimachia nummularia (creeping jenny), 60, 66

M

Madonna lily (*Lilium Candidum*), 60, 99
maiden pink (*Dianthus deltoides*), 124
maintenance of gardens, 27, 28–29
Malus pumila (*M. domestica*) 'Anna' (Anna apple), 112, 131
marigold, 37, 87
    pot (*Calendula officinalis*; calendula), 94
marjoram, sweet (*Origanum majorana*), 141
meadow grasses, Italian, 39
medicinal plants, 33
medlar (*Mespilus germanica*), 114, 135
Melissa officinalis (lemon balm), 112, 132

Mentha
    pulegium var. erecta (pennyroyal mint), 61, 133
    rotundifolia [*M. suaveolens*] (apple mint), 133
    spicata (spearmint), 134
    x piperita (peppermint), 132
Mespilus germanica (medlar), 114, 135
mint, 112
    apple mint (*Mentha rotundifolia* [*M. suaveolens*]), 133
    catmint (*Nepeta x faassenii*), 112, 136
    pennyroyal mint (*Mentha pulegium var. erecta*), 61, 133
    peppermint (*Mentha x piperita*), 132
    spearmint (*Mentha spicata*), 134
'moonshine' yarrow (*Achillea* 'Moonshine'), 116
morning glory, 39
    bush (*Convolvulus cneorum*), 45
    ground (*Convolvulus sabatius* [*C. mauritanicus*]), 96
    Moroccan, 114
Moroccan bindweed, 37
Moroccan morning glory, 114
mother of thyme (*Thymus serpyllum*; creeping thyme), 151
mullein, 87
    nettle-leaved (*Verbascum thapsus*), 108
    woolly (*Verbascum bombyciferum* 'Arctic Summer'),
      152–153
myrtle, 60, 84
    (*Myrtus communis* 'Boetica'), 101
    dwarf myrtle, 39, 60, 89
Myrtus communis 'Boetica' (myrtle), 101

N
Narcissus, 27
    papyraceus (paper whites), 87, 102, 111
    'sp. 'King Alfred' (daffodil), 101
National Archaeological Museum, Naples, 23
Nepeta x faassenii (catmint), 112, 136
Nerium oleander (oleander), 27, 37, 39, 84, 86, 102, 114
nettle-leaved mullein (*Verbascum thapsus*), 108
Neuerburg, Norman, 24–25
nymphaea (artificial grottoes), in Roman gardens, 13–14, 15
Nymphaea sp. (water lily), 40, 56–57, 69, 111, 137

O
oak trees
    cork (*Quercus suber*), 38, 52, 114
    holm, 38
Observations sur les antiquités de la ville d'Herculaneum (Cochin
    and Bellicard), 61
Ocimum basilicum (sweet basil), 112, 137
Olea europaea 'Swan Hill' (Swan Hill olive), 39, 112, 138–139
oleander (*Nerium oleander*), 27, 37, 39, 84, 86, 102, 114
olive, Swan Hill (*Olea europaea* 'Swan Hill'), 39, 112, 138–139
oregano (*Origanum vulgare*), 141
oriental plane tree (*Platanus orientalis*), 18, 70
Origanum
    dictamnus (dittany of Crete), 140
    majorana (sweet marjoram), 141
    vulgare (oregano), 141
ornamental kale (*Brassica oleracea*), 120
oscilli, in Roman gardens, 16
Outdoor Theater, 39
Outer Peristyle Garden
    arbors, 84–85
    circular seats in, 84
    colonnade, 83

    flower colors, range of, 87
    hedging in, 27
    lattice work alcoves, 85
    maintenance of, 28–29
    map of, 34–35
    ocean view from, 89
    plantings and features, overview of, 83–89
    plant species, 90–109
    sculptures, 83, 85, 86–87
    soil of, 28
    Villa architecture echoed in, 27
    water features, 28, 83–84
ox-eye daisy, 87

P
paint colors, for garden benches, lights, and fixtures, 28
Palladius, 20–21
Palla Studio, 70
palm
    date (*Phoenix dactylifera*), 103, 114
      in Getty Villa gardens, 85
      in Roman gardens, 18, 85
    European fan (*Chamaerops humilis*), 27, 38, 86, 95
paper whites (*Narcissus papyraceus*), 87, 102, 111
papyrus (*Cyperus papyrus*), 111–112, 124
Parthenocissus tricuspidata (Boston ivy), 39, 51
pathways, materials for, 28
pea, perennial (*Lathyrus latifolius*), 50
peach (*Prunus persica*), 111, 143
peach-leaved bellflower (*Campanula persicifolia*), 87, 95
pear, European (*Pyrus communis*), 112, 144
pennyroyal mint (*Mentha pulegium var. erecta*), 61, 133
peplophoroi (*peplos* wearers), 59
peppermint (*Mentha x piperita*), 132
perennial pea (*Lathyrus latifolius*), 50
pergolas, in Roman gardens, 12
peristyle gardens, 11
periwinkle (*Vinca major*), 39, 55, 114
perlette grape (*Vitis vinifera* 'Perlette'), 109, 114
Peruvian squill (*Scilla peruviana*), 71, 79
Phoenix dactylifera (date palm), 103, 114
    in Getty Villa Gardens, 85
    in Roman gardens, 18, 85
pinax (pinakes), in Roman gardens, 16
pincushion flower (*Scabiosa columbaria* 'Butterfly Blue';
    small scabious), 60, 67
pine trees (*Pinus*), 39
    Canary Island (*Pinus canariensis*), 38, 51, 114
    Italian stone pine (*Pinus pinea*; umbrella pine), 27, 38,
      111, 142
Pinus. *See* pine trees
Piso, Lucius Calpurnius, 24
plane tree
    London (*Platanus x acerifolia* 'Columbia'), 70, 76
    oriental (*Platanus orientalis*), 18, 70
planters, color of, 28
plants
    in Getty Villa gardens
      selection of, to echo Roman varieties, 27
      sources of, 27
    in Roman gardens, 16–21
      arrangement of, 17
Platanus orientalis (oriental plane tree), 18, 70
Platanus racemosa (California sycamore), 37, 89, 104

Platanus x acerifolia 'Columbia' (London plane tree), 70, 76
Pliny the Elder, 18, 20, 21, 25
Pliny the Younger, 12
plum
    damson, 112
    Prunus x domestica, 143
Poisson, Abel-François, 61
pomegranate (*Punica granatum*), 27, 84, 105, 112
pools. *See* water features
pot marigold (*Calendula officinalis*; calendula), 94
pride of Madeira (*Echium candicans [E. fastuosum]*), 39, 48
Prunus persica (peach), 112, 143
Prunus x domestica (plum), 143
Punica granatum (pomegranate), 27, 84, 105, 112
Pyrus communis (European pear), 112, 144

Q
Quercus suber (cork oak), 38, 52, 114
quince (*Cydonia oblonga*), 112–113, 123

R
radish (*Raphanus sativus*), 144
Ranch House, 40
Raphanus sativus (radish), 144
redwood
    coast, 37, 40
    Sierra, 40
Roman chamomile (*Chamaemelum nobile*; *Anthemis nobilis*),
    112, 121
Roman gardens, 11–21
    architectural and sculptural decoration in, 12–13
    design of, 11
    garden spaces and uses, 11–12
    as model for Getty Villa gardens, 11 (*See also* Villa dei
    Papiri)
    nymphaea (artificial grottoes) in, 13–14
    plants in, 16–21
    statuary in, 15, 16
    topiaries in, 18–20
    water features in, 11, 15–16, 24
    water management in, 11, 12, 15–16, 24
Roman villas, characteristics of, 23
Rosa. *See* rose
rose (*Rosa*), 112
    apothecary's (*Rosa gallica officinalis*), 113
    ballerina musk (*Rosa 'Ballerina'*), 53
    Corsican. *See* Corsican hellebore
    damask (*Rosa 'Autumn Damask'*), 85–86, 106
    gloria mundi (*Rosa 'Gloria mundi'*), 145
    in Roman gardens, 18
    Scepter'd Isle (*Rosa 'Scepter'd Isle'*), 53
rose campion (*Lychnis coronaria*), 87, 100
rosemary (*Rosmarinus officinalis*), 27, 37, 60, 84, 112, 113,
    114, 145
    Tuscan blue (*Rosmarinus officinalis 'Tuscan Blue'*), 106
Rosmarinus officinalis (rosemary), 27, 37, 60, 84, 112, 113,
    114, 145
    'Tuscan Blue' (Tuscan blue rosemary), 106
ruscus (*Ruscus*)
    aculeatus (butcher's broom), 27, 60, 69, 70, 78, 87
    hypoglossum (ruscus), 66, 87

S
sage, 112
    culinary (*Salvia officinalis*), 147
    Jerusalem, 37, 39
    silver (*Salvia argentea*), 146
St. John's wort, 39, 112
Salvia
    argentea (silver sage), 146
    officinalis (culinary sage), 147
Santolina rosmarinifolia [S. virens] (green lavender cotton), 54
Scabiosa columbaria 'Butterfly Blue' (small scabious;
    pincushion flower), 60, 67
scabious, 87
    small (*Scabiosa columbaria* 'Butterfly Blue'; pincushion
    flower), 60, 67
scale of gardens, 27
Scepter'd Isle rose (*Rosa 'Scepter'd Isle'*), 53
Scilla peruviana (Peruvian squill), 71, 79
screens, in Roman gardens, 12–13
sculpture
    at Getty Villa gardens
        as copies of Villa dei Papiri works, 25, 28, 69, 83, 85,
        86–87, 111
        East Garden, 70
        Herb Garden, 111–112
        Inner Peristyle Garden, 59, 60–61
        Outer Peristyle Garden, 83, 85, 86–87
        placement of, 25, 28, 59
    in Roman gardens, 12–13, 15, 16
    at Villa dei Papiri, 23, 24–25
        copies of, at Getty Villa, 25, 28, 69, 83, 85, 86–87, 111
sea pink (*Armeria maritima*), 112, 118
Serbian bellflower (*Campanula poscharskyana*), 62, 87
shade, in Roman gardens, 18, 20
shrubs, in Roman gardens, 16, 18
Siberian iris, 59
Sierra redwood, 40
silver sage (*Salvia argentea*), 146
small scabious (*Scabiosa columbaria* 'Butterfly Blue';
    pincushion flower), 60, 67
smoke bushes, 39
snowflake, 60, 70
Soleirolia soleirolii (baby's tears), 67
Spanish broom, 112
Spanish lavender (*Lavandula stoechas*), 128–129
spearmint (*Mentha spicata*), 134
spurge (*Euphorbia characias wulfenii*), 49
Stachys byzantina (lamb's ear), 148
stone pine, Italian (*Pinus pinea*; umbrella pine), 27, 38, 111, 142
strawberry tree (*Arbutus unedo*), 38, 71, 93
Swan Hill olive (*Olea europaea* 'Swan Hill'), 39, 112, 138–139
sweet basil (*Ocimum basilicum*), 112, 137
sweet broom, 112
sweet marjoram (*Origanum majorana*), 141
sweet violet (*Viola odorata*), 81
sycamore, California (*Platanus racemosa*), 37, 89, 104
symmetry
    in Getty Villa gardens, 27
    in Roman gardens, 11

T

Tanacetum parthenium (feverfew), 70, 80
tarragon (*Artemisia dracunculus*), 119
Teucrium chamaedrys (*T. x lucidrys*; germander), 87, 112, 149
Theater Plaza, 39
themes of garden, statuary and, 16
thyme (*Thymus*), 61, 70, 84, 112
   caraway (*T. herba-barona*), 150–151
   common (*T. vulgaris*), 151
   creeping (mother of thyme; *T. serpyllum*), 151
   lemon-scented (*T. pulegioides* 'Bertram Anderson'), 150
   woolly (*T. pseudolanuginosus*), 151
Thymus. See thyme
tickseed (*Coreopsis lanceolata*), 46
toadflax (*Linaria purpurea*), 87, 99
topiaries
   in Getty Villa gardens, 27
   in Roman gardens, 18–20
"topiarized" trees and shrubs, in Getty Villa gardens, 27
trees, in Roman gardens, 18
trellises, in Roman gardens, 12–13
tulip, lady (*Tulipa clusiana*), 87, 107
Tulipa clusiana (lady tulip), 87, 107
Tuscan blue rosemary (*Rosmarinus officinalis* 'Tuscan Blue'), 106

U

umbrella pine (*Pinus pinea*; Italian stone pine), 27, 38, 111, 142

V

valerian, 112
Varro, 25
Verbascum
   bombyciferum 'Arctic Summer' (woolly mullein), 152–153
   thapsus (nettle-leaved mullein), 108
villa, Roman, characteristics of, 23
Villa dei Papiri (Villa of the Papyri; Herculaneum)
   birdbaths at, 61
   design and construction of, 24
   excavation of, 23–24
   history of, 24
   as model for Getty Villa, 11, 23
      contemporary requirements and, 25
      East Garden, 69
      Entry Path, 37
      Herb Garden, 111
      Inner Peristyle Garden, 59
      Outer Peristyle Garden, 83
   sculpture displayed at, 23, 24–25
      copies of, at Getty Villa, 25, 28, 69, 83, 85, 86–87, 111
Villa of Hadrian (Tivoli), 15
Villa of Poppaea (Oplontis), 16, 18
Villa of Publius Fannius Synistor (Boscoreale), 12
Villa San Marco (Stabiae), 15, 69
Villas at Boscoreale, 12
Vinca major (periwinkle), 39, 55, 114
vines, in Roman gardens, 20
Viola, 60, 70
   odorata (sweet violet), 81
violets, 60, 84, 87, 113
   sweet (*Viola odorata*), 81
vistas
   of ocean, from Outer Peristyle Garden, 89

in Roman gardens, 11
Vitis vinifera 'Perlette' (perlette grape), 109, 114

W

wallflower (*Erysimum cheiri*; *Cheiranthus cheiri*), 97, 114
water features, 28
   East Garden, 28, 69–70
   Herb Garden, 28, 111
   Inner Peristyle Garden, 28, 59, 61
   Outer Peristyle Garden, 28, 83–84
   in Roman gardens, 11, 15–16, 24
   at Villa dei Papiri, 24
watering, guidelines for, 33
water irises, 69, 75, 76
water lily (*Nymphaea sp.*), 40, 56–57, 69, 111, 137
water management
   in Getty Villa gardens, 29
   in Roman gardens, 11, 12, 15–16, 24
   at Villa dei Papiri, 24
Weber, Karl, 24, 61, 111
weeping wall, along Entry Path, 40
white iris (*Iris germanica* 'Florentina'), 84, 97
windflower (*Anemone coronaria*), 87, 92
winter gem boxwood (*Buxus microphylla koreana* 'Winter Gem'), 94
woody plants, in Roman gardens, 16–17
woolly mullein (*Verbascum bombyciferum* 'Arctic Summer'), 152–153
woolly thyme (*Thymus pseudolanuginosus*), 151
woolly yarrow (*Achillea tomentosa* 'Maynard's Gold' [*A. tomentosa 'Aurea'*]), 91

Y

yarrow (*Achillea*), 37, 87, 112
   'moonshine' (*Achillea* 'Moonshine'), 116
   woolly (*Achillea tomentosa* 'Maynard's Gold' [*A. tomentosa 'Aurea'*]), 91
yellow citron (*Citrus medica* 'Etrog'), 113, 122
yellow flag iris (*Iris pseudacorus*), 76